MW01178516

OZZIE'S SCHOOL OF MANAGEMENT

OZZIE'S
SCHOOL OF MANAGEMENT

LESSONS FROM THE DUGOUT, THE CLUBHOUSE, AND THE DOGHOUSE

RICK MORRISSEY

TIMES BOOKS HENRY HOLT AND COMPANY NEW YORK

Times Books
Henry Holt and Company, LLC
Publishers since 1866
175 Fifth Avenue
New York, New York 10010

Library of Congress Cataloging-in-Publication Data

Morrissey, Rick.
Ozzie's school of management : lessons from the dugout, the clubhouse, and the doghouse / Rick Morrissey.
p. cm.
Includes index.
ISBN 978-0-8050-9500-5 (hardback)
1. Guillen, Ozzie. 2. Baseball managers—United States—Biography. I. Title.
GV865.G84M67 2012
796.357092—dc23
[B] 2011049604

Henry Holt books are available for special promotions and premiums. For details contact: Director, Special Markets.

First Edition 2012

Designed by Kelly S. Too

Printed in the United States of America
1 3 5 7 9 10 8 6 4 2

For Anne

CONTENTS

OZZIE'S SCHOOL OF MANAGEMENT

• INTRODUCTION •

CREATE A MISSION STATEMENT

> *"Every day you've got to be in that bullfighting ring, and be careful now because that motherfucking bull is going to get your ass."*
>
> —Ozzie Guillen, May 19, 2011

Ozzie Guillen's favorite sport is not baseball. It's bullfighting. Although the gabby manager of the Miami Marlins can and will talk about anything for hours, his voice becomes more expressive and his arms start moving like a juggler's when he talks about the bloody showdowns between matadors and bulls.

If he could redo his life, he says, he would start over as a bullfighter in his native Venezuela. This makes perfect sense, even though he has won a World Series as a manager, even though he is one of the most popular people in major-league baseball, and even though the sport has made him millions of dollars.

To Guillen, bullfighting is different, elemental, noble. The way a matador holds the attention of the crowd, the way he carries himself. Such style! Such bravery! He toys with the bull, plays with its mind, works it like a confidence man working a mark. He kneels theatrically in front of the beast to the great amusement of the crowd. In the way the bull can't take its eyes off the cape, the people in the arena can't take their eyes off the bullfighter. One bad decision and the matador is a gored rag doll.

In terms of sheer balls-of-steel courage, what are other sports compared with that? Bullshit, that's what.

Oh, this is made for Ozzie Guillen, who believes a good baseball manager commands attention, if for no other reason than to protect his players from the pointy horns of public criticism. And so he stands in the ring as the twelve-hundred-pound bull makes charge after charge. The bull can be his critics. The bull can be baseball officials, his general manager, or a world that doesn't understand him. But he stands with one hand on his hip, chin held dismissively high, and dares all of them to bring it on.

It's better to be the bullfighter than the bull, though being the bullfighter isn't a walk in the park. If there's a principle with which Ozzie attacks life, that would be it.

Unless it's this: The tongue is mightier than the sword that finally pierces the bull's heart.

Ah, Guillen's tongue. It is razor sharp. It has made him famous. But that tongue can also be the instrument of his death, career-wise. It certainly hastened his departure from Chicago, where he had managed the White Sox for eight seasons.

Whenever Guillen says he wishes he were a bullfighter, his son Ozzie Jr. rolls his eyes.

"Dad, do you know if you were a bullfighter, you'd be dead?"

"What do you mean?"

"During a baseball game, you say hi to everyone you see," Ozzie Jr. says. "In the bullfight, you'd say hi to someone and you'd be gone."

Ozzie Sr. has to admit his boy has a point. If he were busy waving to bullfighting fans, that motherfucking bull certainly would get his ass.

Ozzie's mission statement: Don't take your eye off the bull.

The bull appeared to be a contract extension, but it was so many more things than that. The exasperating White Sox were coming down to the last month of the 2011 season, and Guillen, their banty rooster of a manager, informed reporters that he wouldn't be back the following season unless team chairman Jerry Reinsdorf added more years to a deal that ran out after the 2012 season.

It was a bold, outrageous, Ozzie-like statement. It was ill-timed and selfish, considering the Sox were still alive in the American League Central Division race. But it was also a calculated business tactic from a man who needed to find out how much he was wanted. He saw a window that would soon close. And given that he had always been like a chatty tour-bus guide, it never occurred to him that he wouldn't bring everyone along for the ride with his contract demands.

The root of all this late-season evil wasn't money. Or, if it was about money, it was about money as a way to fill a hole or salve a wound.

As much as anything, it was about the need to feel needed. Guillen and the White Sox general manager, Kenny Williams, had clashed for years. Both men were close to Reinsdorf. It was a sibling rivalry without shared blood. Guillen came from a broken home and looked upon the chairman as a father figure. Reinsdorf had seen management qualities in Williams years before he hired him as the team's general manager.

Whom did Reinsdorf like best? One way to keep score is with contract security.

Guillen was keeping score.

He knew the Marlins likely were waiting for him with a multiyear contract. They had tried to hire him the year before, and it was no secret they would be in hot pursuit again. The team would be opening a new ballpark in Miami in 2012, and what better way to christen it than with an extremely high-profile Venezuelan manager in a heavily Latino city?

If any manager could help put butts in seats in a town that hadn't shown much passion for baseball, it was Guillen, a yapping, exuberant, combative, restless, relentlessly foul-mouthed ball of energy. He's the Charles Barkley of baseball, but with a position of responsibility and authority. Scary but true. The Florida job would not be open long. Which team, Guillen wanted to know, loved him more?

There are different kinds of leaders. And then there is Ozzie, whose management style is more suited to a mosh pit than a boardroom. He always figured he'd find another job easily if it didn't end well for him with the White Sox.

He figured right.

"There are a lot of horseshit managers out there that are given two and three shots to manage in the big leagues," he said before the 2011 season began. "I don't see why not me."

In the past, locked in a boxer's clinch, Guillen and Williams would peer over the edge of disaster and see the bottom far below. And just before they fell and hurtled toward sure professional death, they'd let go of each other, dust themselves off, and at least give the appearance of shaking hands.

Was that any way to work? No, it wasn't. It was a dynamic that shouldn't have succeeded but did for a long time. Management types are supposed to be of the same mind and on the same page most of the time.

In a Harvard Business School world of management, Guillen's loose approach makes absolutely no sense. But from the practical standpoint of working with a baseball team it does. Williams would have preferred understatement in his manager, but for the most part, he understood that there was a certain structure to Guillen's chaos. You had to squint to see it sometimes, but it was there.

Part of life is knowing when to move on. Guillen played thirteen seasons with the White Sox in the 1980s and 1990s and had managed eight more. He loved the Sox as much as a professional in a cold sports world can love a team. But the often-contentious relationship with Williams had crumbled, in part, over tension involving Guillen's sons, and nothing—nothing—was more important to the manager than his family.

Fatigue had set in as well. The Sox weren't winning, fans were bone-tired of the Ozzie-Kenny drama, and Guillen had heard enough criticism to last a lifetime.

How could a man in need of love find it in any of that?

Reinsdorf rejected Guillen's extension request and allowed him to walk away from the final year of his contract with the White Sox. He might love Guillen like a son and might forever be in his debt for the manager's victory in the 2005 World Series, but he wasn't going to give him a contract extension. Not after a sub-.500 season that was supposed to be so much more.

In the end, though, it was Ozzie's call. He made a cold business decision with his head, not with the warm heart that used to beat only for the White Sox. A multiyear contract told Guillen who loved him most.

So the woeful, last-place Marlins? A man who grew up painfully poor in Venezuela could learn to love the Marlins for $10 million over four years. Oh, he most certainly could, despite his earlier observation in 2011 that the citizens of Miami are "fake." Best of all, he wouldn't be sitting on the hot seat that would have awaited him in Chicago in 2012.

The same fieriness that had caused an untold number of outbursts and seemingly endless controversy over the years was the same fieriness that pushed him out the door in Chicago. He simply couldn't work where he didn't feel vitally wanted.

So it was Ozzie to the Marlins, who would give the White Sox two minor-league players as compensation. He managed his last game for the Sox on September 26, 2011. Two days later, on a brilliantly sunny day in Miami, Marlins owner Jeffrey Loria introduced Guillen as the team's new manager. Until then, Loria had been best known for (a) not spending money on players and (b) yelling at umpires from his box seats near the Marlins dugout.

Note to Loria: Neither of those things meshes with Ozzie's management style.

Only time will tell whether Guillen's need for attention, for being the bullfighter alone with the bull in the ring, will be satisfied in Miami, where attendance was the lowest in the National League for seven straight seasons, including 2011.

"I own Chicago," Guillen said several years ago, and he wasn't wrong. Can he own Miami? Not with LeBron James and Dwyane Wade around, but everyone will know he's living there because of raised decibel levels. There are two words that, as far as anyone knows, have never escaped his lips in tandem: "No comment."

The odds are that it probably won't end well in South Florida, or anywhere, for the volatile Guillen. The same issues that arose in Chicago—family, trust, the longing for appreciation—likely will arise again. But the same man who lit up Chicago with his personality will do the same in Miami.

The change of venue doesn't change much. He still has the attention of people all over the country who appreciate boyish enthusiasm, who recognize a forty-eight-year-old wild child when he's stomping around in their midst, and who like their vulgarity to have a certain meter to it. The people who despise him, no small number, can't help peeking in his direction.

Ozzie's Ozzie. The wild ride continues. The American League has been duly entertained. Now it's the National League's turn.

Whatever happens going forward with Guillen is an unwritten story, but he brings a body of work with him to Miami. It's full of ink blotches, and there's a lot of scribbling in the margins. But he does business a certain way, and that's not going to change because of a change of climate. He's going to manage people the way he always has.

Go back to an incident in June 2010. The sticky-sweet fragrance of burning incense is wafting from Guillen's clubhouse office, as it often does. It's meant to calm him, to quiet him, to make him more meditative, but it's useless. It's like shushing a blaring radio and hoping it takes a vow of silence. To date, nothing has stopped him from speaking or from speaking his mind. It's as if he walks around with a truth serum IV drip.

On this day, the White Sox' twenty-three-year-old second baseman Gordon Beckham has committed a cardinal sin in the Book of Ozzie. He has sat in front of his locker and slouched, a portrait of defeat, *The Thinker* in utter despair. He has been struggling horribly at the plate for the better part of three months, and nothing he or anybody else has done has gotten him out of it.

Guillen can abide hitting slumps; he can't abide the physical act of sitting and slumping. He dispatches his bench coach, Joey Cora, to deliver Beckham to the boss's office. This boss has an approach unlike any other boss in America.

It is time for an Ozzie Guillen pep talk, using every variation of one of the first words he learned when he came to the United States from Venezuela thirty years ago. Welcome to Ozzie's School of Management.

"Listen, motherfucker, I told you one fucking thing," Guillen begins. "I don't care if you're 0-for-fucking-40. I don't give a fuck you make errors. Next time I see you with your fucking head down, you get the fuck to the minor leagues. Okay? I trust you. Get your fucking head up and fucking play the way you should be playing. And fuck everything else."

File that under Ozzie Management Commandment No. 5: Be Nurturing, No Matter How Much It Hurts. The best workplace managers communicate well with their employees, especially newer ones. And, really, isn't that what Guillen was doing with Beckham? Communicating, in the language of his particular world and his particular workplace?

The Marlins had the third-youngest team in the majors in 2011. Guillen will seek out the young players on the roster and take them on as his projects. It's what he does. He will counsel them, encourage them, and get in their faces if they don't play hard all the time. They'd be wise to pay attention.

If you're within earshot of Guillen, which is to say within

about a half mile, you have to listen, for one simple reason: you might miss something. Something outrageous. Something illuminating. Something contradictory. Something fun. Something nonsensical. Something that might get you out of a slump.

Something.

Not long after that chat, Beckham broke out, hitting .354 in the month of July. He had walked out of the meeting in June uplifted. How could that be when, by all rights, he should have been treated for burns after feeling Ozzie's wrath?

"He's a mess, but we love him," Beckham had said. "He's a fun mess."

He is that. He's a motivator. He's a freethinker and a freer talker. He's part psychologist, part strategist, part friend to the players, part pain in the ass. He's a wholly unique mess.

And to the everlasting gratitude of people tired of cold, distant sports figures, he's a mess who adores the spotlight. In Chicago, one of the biggest spotlights of the year arrives when the White Sox and the Cubs play each other in two three-game interleague series. Guillen loved the fact that the two sides of town despise each other when it comes to baseball. It was right in his wheelhouse. The North Side Cubs are the team for conspicuous consumers, the South Side Sox for blue-collar folk. The Cubs have the bigger fan base and receive more attention. The White Sox have the more recent World Series title—2005 to the Cubs' carbon-dated 1908.

Every season, Ozzie would come to venerable Wrigley Field and refer to it as a hovel, irritating Cubs fans. It probably didn't advance the cause of peace when, a few years back, he said that rats lived inside the old ballpark and that, judging by their size, they appeared to be on a weight-lifting program.

But he has moved on. Who's going to be his twelve-hundred-pound bull now? The Mets and their underperforming payroll? The Phillies and their All-Star pitching staff? The Braves and their pedigree?

Somebody, count on it.

In an increasingly packaged sport, where people sand down their opinions into smooth, inoffensive sound bites, Ozzie is the rough, uncut truth. Or at least his version of it, and he doesn't leave much room for his mind to be changed.

"People say, 'You've got to call him and talk to him. He's got to knock this off,'" says ESPN baseball analyst John Kruk, a former minor-league teammate of Guillen's. "I say, 'I would never do that.' That's what made him what he is. That's why he is where he is, a successful person, because he's not afraid. He's not afraid to speak his mind. He's not afraid to tell you how he feels. Is it something that everyone wants to hear? No. But is it something he wants to say and he's passionate about? Yep. Say it."

Guillen says what he means and means what he says—at least at the moment he's saying it.

He respects former St. Louis Cardinals manager Tony La Russa, the successful, puffed-up skipper who was the manager of the White Sox when Guillen broke in as a player in 1985. He really, really does. But . . .

"It's about the players," Guillen says. "A lot of people say, 'Well, Tony, he got two thousand, three thousand wins.' Fuck, he's been managing for thirty years. That's because of players."

Pro sports are all about the players, but there's no doubt who the maximum leader is on a Guillen team. From time to time, his players experience temporary amnesia on this subject. Ozzie has his own way of reminding them who is in charge.

It sometimes feels like a scene from the film *GoodFellas*.

"They're always going to challenge you, test you," he says. "I tell one of my pitchers, 'You've got a fucking problem?' He says no. I say, 'Oh, because I think you look at me funny.' If I don't confront him, everybody else says, 'This motherfucker's got an attitude, and Ozzie don't say anything.'

"I told Freddy Garcia. I told fucking Jon Garland. I told Mark Buehrle, 'You got a fucking problem?' I told Tadahito Iguchi, 'If you got a fucking problem with me, then fucking tell me. Then we'll fucking figure it out.' I'm not afraid. If you respect me, I'll respect you back.

"You don't like me because I take you out of the game? Well, don't make me fucking take you out. You think I fucking want to take you out? You think I want to pinch-hit for you? You think I want to bench you? That happened with Carl Everett. I put him down to batting seventh, and he got pissed. Well, Carl, you fucking think I want to put you seventh? Our club is better when you're batting third, motherfucker. Don't blame me. Blame your fucking self."

Honesty is a dwindling natural resource, but Guillen has deep reserves of the stuff. On the eve of Opening Day in 2011, big, fluffy snowflakes had floated down and congregated on the grass at Progressive Field in Cleveland. Guillen had looked at the snow-globe scene and said what everybody outside of Anchorage had been thinking—that beginning a baseball season in early April in a cold-weather city is "very stupid." Did Major League Baseball have something against Ozzie's Sox? Or was it that someone in the commissioner's office thought frostbite builds character? Hey, so do harmful UV rays in California and Florida.

But Guillen was the one who said it was "very stupid." Nobody else. Nobody says anything anymore.

"He doesn't have an off button sometimes," White Sox catcher A. J. Pierzynski said. "Sometimes he needs a mute button. And there are days where people put a quarter in him and wind him up, and he'll go forever. But that's Ozzie. That's why people love Ozzie."

Issues over Guillen's family almost tore the White Sox apart in 2010, eventually pitting Guillen against Williams in what became a national soap opera. Guillen forced his twenty-four-year-old son Oney to resign from his position in the team's video-scouting department after Oney criticized the front office on his Twitter account.

But that wasn't the end of the matter. Before the 2011 season, Oney Guillen tweeted that the former White Sox closer Bobby Jenks had drinking and marital problems. Why would Oney do such a thing? Because Jenks had signed as a free agent with the Boston Red Sox and told reporters that he was happy to now be playing for a manager, Terry Francona, "who knows how to run a bullpen," a clear shot at Ozzie. No one throws a stone at a Guillen without another Guillen lobbing a grenade as a commensurate response.

Jenks responded by diagnosing Oney Guillen with classic middle-child syndrome. But Ozzie told reporters he wasn't mad.

"I wish I was mad about it because I will rip his throat [out]," the 170-pound Guillen said of the 275-pound Jenks.

It's not the sort of thing you'd hear from New York Yankees manager Joe Girardi.

At the beginning of spring training, Guillen had insisted there wouldn't be conflict on Planet Ozzie in 2011.

"[This season] will be quiet," he said. "I promised myself and my family it will be boring. . . . Of course I'm going to be mad [at times]. But I try to stay away from drama."

Nobody believed him. Nobody should have. Oney would keep tweeting provocative thoughts, and so would Ozzie. A few of the dad's tweets appeared during a White Sox game at Yankee Stadium, which would lead to a suspension and a hefty fine from Major League Baseball. A coffeemaker in the visiting manager's office in Toronto would suffer a violent death after a bad White Sox loss. So would a chair.

No one in his or her right mind should believe 2012 or beyond will be drama-free for Ozzie Guillen in Miami. No one should want it to be.

What would the world be like if everyone were as open as he is? Either a lot more interesting or decimated by nuclear missiles. One or the other.

He's in the perfect job for him, a job that requires conversing with people. Hell for Ozzie Guillen is a gag order.

Heaven is a baseball season and an audience.

·1·

ALL MEN ARE CREATED EQUAL, IN THEORY

An older gentleman stood near the dugout at U.S. Cellular Field, the home of the White Sox, between innings of a game against the Oakland Athletics in June 2011. His seat was far away from where he was now standing. Joey Cora, the bench coach, had watched the man make his way purposefully down one of the aisles in the premium box seats.

Ozzie Guillen likes to stand on the top step of the dugout in part so he can take in the crowd while he's working. To put yourself in the line of fire of fan abuse would seem to be masochistic, but Ozzie isn't like most other major-league managers. He wants to hear and be heard, to see and be seen. Every baseball game is a happening for him, an experience, and part of that is the interaction with the fans. To sequester himself would be like U2 choosing to play a concert in a garage.

And Ozzie would have no one to talk to when he got bored.

Now the old man was saying something, and Guillen could tell by the earnest expression on his face and the way he leaned over the railing that it was important, or at least important to him. But with the music pounding from the stadium's loudspeakers, Guillen couldn't make out the words.

"What's he saying?" he asked Cora.

"He's saying that Dunn needs to go to the eye doctor," Cora said.

"He just hit a fucking home run!" Guillen boomed.

Ozzie was laughing now, a big improvement over his mood of a few innings earlier, when the home crowd had stood and cheered after Adam Dunn had been hit by a pitch. That's how bad things had gotten for the Sox' designated hitter, a $56 million free-agent signing in the off-season. It was a cheer slathered with derision. *Dunn finally has found a way to get on base! If it takes a 90 mph fastball to the elbow to get him there, we're all for it!*

It had been a miserable first two months of the season for the hulking home run hitter. His batting average was a sickly .178, and he had spent most of his time picking dirt off his uniform from the deep hole he had dug for himself. After each strikeout—and there had been lots of them—the crowd booed him as if he were guilty of war crimes.

At its heart, managing is not about poring over statistics during games and making the perfect move at the perfect moment. It's not about deciding when to bring in a reliever or when to change the batting order. There's a romanticized image of the major-league manager as a steely-eyed strategist and master move-maker who relies on a treasure trove of statistical data to outwit his opponent. That's part of managing, the way sliding a cake into an oven is part of making a cake. What Guillen had to do in dealing with Dunn—show unflinching faith through bits of thick and loads of thin—that's managing. It's dealing with human beings who have feelings, families, bad days, money problems, large egos, and torturous doubts. It's dealing with different players in different ways.

It's doing things behind the scenes that have nothing to do with whether a right-handed hitter does well against a particular left-handed pitcher whenever the relative humidity is at 57.8 percent in the seventh inning. It's managing people, not numbers.

It's leaving open the possibility you might be wrong and pushing forward anyway, shoulder down, into the gale. It's doing it with a flair that only Guillen possesses.

So this fan standing there wanting the manager to schedule an eye appointment for his slumping slugger? Ozzie listened, and he didn't listen. He laughed and waved to the man. He took it in and ignored it, just as he had ignored the wall of sound that had been pleading for Dunn's benching for weeks.

Guillen refused to desert Dunn, which is exactly how he viewed a potential benching—as a desertion, a betrayal. If he didn't stand up for his player, he risked losing him. He was convinced that most managers, if they had been in his position, would have caved in to public pressure and taken Dunn out of the lineup.

This was a case of spine over matter. Ozzie would take his lumps, and there would be a lot of them, although he didn't know that as he laughed at the fan. The season would swirl toward the drain partly because of Dunn, and Guillen's reputation would take a beating. But the manager refused to budge. In hindsight, it would have been better if he had budged and sent Dunn to the bench.

Ozzie knows a place where you can stick your hindsight.

"There are a lot of managers who worry about what the fuck fans are going to say or that they're going to be criticized because of a move," he said. "And they don't worry about the real thing. The real thing is the player. If you kick the players in the ass because you're afraid of the fans booing you or what the media is going to say, then you're losing three things. You're losing the fans, you're losing the media, and you're losing your players.

"The most important thing is your player. He's the one who's going to perform for you. He's going to make you look good, or he's going to make you look bad. Believe me, 90 percent of the managers out there, they try to protect their ass instead of doing what they're supposed to do. I don't give a shit what they say. I played baseball. I know what those managers are doing."

One day, when Dunn was at his lowest, Guillen called him into his office. The manager had a fine line to walk. He wanted to let Dunn know he supported him, but he didn't want to make him feel as if he were overly worried about him, even though he most certainly was. What he wanted to convey more than anything was that he had no doubt Dunn would get back to being the player he had been the previous seven years, the monster at the plate who had averaged 40 home runs and 101 runs batted in. Of this one thing, Guillen was absolutely certain. That sort of productivity doesn't just disappear forever.

"Don't try to be our savior," he told Dunn. "You're not our savior. You're our helper. You came here to help us, not save us. You're good. Don't second-guess your abilities. I'm behind you. We're all behind you. If they say something about you, it's my fault. I'm the one who put you out there."

Had this been a player without Dunn's standing and accomplishments, Guillen might not have been so patient. He had taken a similar tack with leadoff hitter Juan Pierre, another veteran who was struggling at the plate and in the field, and it drove White Sox fans insane.

But Guillen believed there was a chance he'd lose his team if he treated Dunn or Pierre the same way he treated someone like Brent Lillibridge, a twenty-seven-year-old Sox outfielder who had spent the previous three seasons bouncing back and forth between the majors and Triple-A. If he gave up on a veteran, it would look like panic.

"I treat people equally with respect," Guillen said. "But equally? No. That's not true. That's a bunch of shit. Every manager has got his favorite players. Every manager gets along with somebody better than others. Like I talk to Mark Buehrle more than I talk to Gavin Floyd. I talk to Alexei Ramirez more than I talk to Paul Konerko.

"Equally with respect? Yes. I don't give a shit if you're making $30 million or you're fucking Lillibridge. I will respect you. But you can't treat people equally. You can't. That's a lie. You're lying."

He's not always so understanding with other players as he was with Dunn. When the reliever Will Ohman had two bad appearances to start the 2011 season, Guillen told reporters the pitcher "needs to get his head out of his ass." It's the kind of statement that, in the past, had left players shaking their heads over Guillen. When he publicly calls out a player, he breaks an unwritten baseball rule: you can rip a player in private all you want, but when you get in front of the media you support him.

Guillen saw this situation as a matter of effort and focus. Dunn and Pierre were trying their hardest. A journeyman reliever like Ohman shouldn't look so lost.

Guillen's lack of a filter is why observers in Miami are braced for possible fireworks between the new manager and the outfielder Logan Morrison. Morrison is a talented player with opinions and a Twitter account that got him into trouble in 2011. In August, the team demoted him to Triple-A because of what it considered distasteful tweets. The tipping point? It could have been the tweet in which he called one of his Twitter followers an "underrated slut." Or it could have been the photo he posted of himself wearing a "Sharktits" T-shirt.

Most likely, it was the tweet with the photo of a hopelessly nerdy man and the accompanying poll, "Is this David Samson? Yes or no? Vote now." Samson happens to be the Marlins' president.

So an inevitable clash looms between Guillen and Morrison, right? Not necessarily. Think of the loud Morrison as a prophet, in a Sharktits T-shirt instead of camel hair clothes, preparing the way for the louder Guillen. Morrison can be as outspoken as he wants to be as long as he can play. That's all Guillen cares about. There's room for everyone's quirkiness in Ozzie's world.

He had very little use for the outfielder Nick Swisher in 2008, not because Swisher seemed almost genetically in need of media attention, but because he hit .219 and moped when he was benched.

If a player mopes or doesn't try hard, he is a dead man to Ozzie. It doesn't matter if he's a star or a rookie. In this sense, Guillen is democratic.

On the same June night that Sox fans were giving Dunn a standing ovation for getting hit by a pitch and Guillen felt like crying for his much-maligned designated hitter, the manager confronted shortstop Alexei Ramirez for jogging, rather than sprinting, to first base after hitting a fly ball to right field. Guillen met him at the dugout steps.

"The next time you do that, you'll be running to Guatemala," he fumed.

Later, in a more reflective mood, he talked about all the meanings that Ramirez's lackadaisical effort had carried with it, even if the Missile, as Guillen referred to the Cuban, didn't intend it that way.

"When you don't run the bases, you don't respect me, you don't respect your teammates, you don't respect the people paying to watch you play," he said.

A few days later, Ozzie the Good Cop was back. The Sox were playing Oakland again, and Guillen had brought in Sergio Santos to pitch the ninth inning with Chicago leading 5–3. Santos had been struggling, having picked up the loss in the previous two games in which he had pitched. Here was a chance to build the reliever's confidence.

Santos started off poorly, giving up a single, striking out a batter, and walking another. Guillen went to the mound to calm him. Santos induced a fly out, then proceeded to give up another hit and a run, cutting the Sox' lead to 5–4. So much for Ozzie's soothing words. Now the Athletics had Coco Crisp coming to the plate with men on first and second and two outs.

Baseball people talk about "the book." There is no such official tome. The book is conventional wisdom. It's tradition, passed down from manager to manager, dealing in best-sense approaches to various situations. It's also statistical probabilities. If you go by the book, you're taking the route that carries with it the most recommendations and, presumably, the least risk.

In this case, the book said to bring in a left-handed pitcher to face the switch-hitting Crisp, who was batting .203 versus lefties and .280 against righties. The book said to hurry up already because it looked as if Santos, a right-hander, was choking.

But Santos needed emotional support, not more bludgeons to his ego. Two years before, after seven years as an infielder with three other organizations, he had joined the Sox' minor-league system and become a pitcher.

A year later, armed with a 95-mph fastball and a hard slider, he was on the Sox' big-league roster as a reliever. Now, with two men on and two out in the ninth inning, he was at something of a crossroads. Guillen loved Santos's attitude, but could he trust him with the closer's role?

Ozzie had a decision to make. His team had clawed back into the division race after a terrible start to the 2011 season. He could take the preferred route and bring in a lefty or he could build some equity in his shaky right-hander.

Guillen decided on a book burning. He wanted Santos to believe that the manager believed. If he brought someone else in from the bullpen, he risked losing Santos forever.

"Then all of a sudden I'm showing him I don't have confidence in him," Guillen said of the move he chose not to make. "Managing and coaching is making sure you give the guys opportunities, put them in the best spot, and believe in them when they're down. It's easy to manage when everybody's good."

Santos induced Crisp to ground out to third. He immediately sought out Guillen to thank him for his faith.

"That did wonders for my confidence," Santos said.

Other managers might have looked at Guillen's decision, shaken their heads, and walked away mumbling to themselves, much as the old man who had suggested Dunn needed an eye exam had done.

But they're not Ozzie, for better or worse.

When he's deciding how to approach certain situations, Guillen riffles through his memories. One of those situations came up in the first game of the 2011 season. Despite the forty-three-degree chill, the Sox were pounding the Indians in Cleveland. Not just beating them, but making their pitchers look like Little Leaguers with self-esteem issues.

In blowouts, managers often pull some of their starters from the game. It's a chance to get some playing time for their bench players. One of those bench players was Omar Vizquel, who would turn forty-four three weeks later. Vizquel is five foot nine and 180 pounds of constant motion who had willed himself into an eleven-time Gold Glove shortstop. He had gotten kicked out of grade school three times in Venezuela for "throwing things at people" and "hitting people with sticks." What says "future Hall of Fame baseball player" more than that?

And now here was Vizquel sitting on the bench as the Sox piled up runs against the Indians. Guillen thought about the sad sight of a former star trudging on to the field to give a younger player a rest in the late innings of a romp. It would have been an insult, the manager thought. Someone of Vizquel's stature needs to be celebrated, not dragged down to human level.

"I don't think any manager should slap a Hall of Fame player doing that," Guillen said. "You're going to lose respect from your team. His teammates are going to say, 'Look at

Ozzie playing Omar.' That's why we have other players. I'd never do it to a player."

That decision had wiggled its way up from Guillen's past. In 2000, he was in his last year in the big leagues, a thirty-six-year-old shortstop on his last baseball legs in Tampa Bay. Manager Larry Rothschild inserted him in the eighth inning of a game the Devil Rays trailed, 17–1.

"I was kind of upset," Guillen said. "I knew it was my job, but in the meanwhile, it's 17–1, goddamn, I paid my dues already. I knew it was my job, and I've got to go play. But goddamn, you think I'm going to be happy with one at-bat? I already have ten thousand at-bats. I don't need one at-bat. They did it to me, and I wasn't as great a player as Omar was."

Guillen never said anything to Rothschild. Took the slight, swallowed it, digested it. And never forgot it.

"What was Larry Rothschild going to say?" Guillen said. "He would have said, 'That's your job. You don't want it? Get the fuck out of here.' But the players were talking about it. Like, 'Why is this guy playing you when we're down seventeen runs?' I never go to the manager asking anything because that's the job I picked. But because I didn't like it, I'm not going to do it to somebody else."

The lesson Guillen took away, aside from the one about not insulting veteran players, was how fragile respect is—how hard it is to get and how easy it is to lose.

It's the manager's job to keep twenty-five plates spinning, which is to say that the manager's job is impossible. There are twenty-five players on each major-league roster, and there are always some who are struggling, no matter how good the player is or how good the team is. At some point in the season, each ballplayer will be on intimate terms with failure. No one is good for 162 games.

For Guillen, that ensures six months of varying degrees of misery. The leadoff hitter might be knocking the yarn out of the baseball, but the guy batting cleanup can't get a hit. Or a pitcher suddenly can't locate the strike zone with GPS.

"Coaches and managers, they don't have a life," Guillen said. "They're lonely because they have to worry about the guy who failed. You got three hits, everybody's happy. This guy wins the game, everybody's happy. It's easy to manage the guys having success. Fuck, anybody can do that. But being next to the guy who failed, being next to the people who need to be helped, that's the hard part.

"We win games and I'm in the back of the plane talking with Carlos Quentin or whoever had a bad game. I know they're down. I sit with them and talk to them. Why? Because I played. Why? Because I went through it. Why? Because I had people around me when I played to teach me that. Whatever you learned, you provide that to other people."

Carlos Quentin. So talented yet so tightly wound that he sometimes looks like he dresses in copper coil rather than cotton clothing. A smile looks as foreign on his face as a doorknob would. Guillen tried to loosen him up. It didn't work.

In the end, he decided to leave the outfielder alone. Everybody's different.

"He can't help it," Guillen said. "We tried it for the last three years, and that's the way he is. I think people have to respect that. People have to understand his point. This is a guy who takes this game very seriously. Sometimes, when you don't take the game too serious, people don't think you care. When you are serious, people think you're too serious. You can't make people happy either way.

"That's the way he grew up. That's the way he's been his whole life. We've talked to him. You cannot change that. We tried a lot. We have fun with him. We try everything, and so far, nothing worked. I told the coaches, let him be himself.

"He's having more fun now than he was the last couple years. I told him, 'Listen, bro, just make sure you enjoy the game because sooner or later, you're not going to play anymore, and you're going to regret it.' "

When intense players are in a slump, Guillen's first impulse is to reach out to help, but he has learned to see their point. Like Quentin, White Sox first baseman Paul Konerko is more serious than relaxed about his craft. He has gone through several severe hitting slumps in which he was his own worst enemy. The more he struggled, the tighter he became, to the point where it was a wonder he could walk to the batter's box.

Guillen once brought him into his office and told him not to take the game so seriously. And then he received an education from Konerko.

"He said, 'Hitting is the only way I can contribute to this ball club. I can't run, I can't throw, and I'm a pretty average fielder. I've got to hit to make my money and to help you,' " Guillen recalled.

Konerko's self-scouting report was fairly accurate. He's a much better first baseman than he was giving himself credit for, but he couldn't outrun a two-toed sloth just off the disabled list. He takes every at-bat as seriously as last rites.

When Konerko laid out what was at stake, when he mentioned how it feels knowing your career is based on one skill, Guillen suddenly understood the pressure his player put on himself. It's the pressure a good hitter with holes in his game feels. It can be suffocating to wonder if the one gift you've been given has left for good.

The opposite had been true of Guillen as a player. He had been a very good shortstop but a .264 lifetime hitter over sixteen seasons, the first thirteen with the White Sox, the last three with the Baltimore Orioles, the Atlanta Braves, and the Tampa Bay Devil Rays. He hadn't felt the pressure to hit that Quentin or Konerko sometimes felt. He was an average hitter, and everyone knew it. There weren't high expectations waiting for him when he arrived at the plate. Fielding was what Guillen did well, and that skill wasn't going to desert him. Hitting slumps arrive for no particular reason, loiter, resist remedies, and often leave as suddenly as they come. There's more control when it comes to fielding.

"When you're in a mental funk, I'm sure he can't understand that," Konerko said. "He just looks at it like, 'I don't get it. I never worried about hitting.' He says, 'I went 0-for-4 my whole career.' I've heard him say that a million times. If I did that, it'd be a very short career."

But when Konerko unburdened himself, it was indeed a lesson for Guillen, who realized he shouldn't presume to know everything that goes through a player's head. And it further reinforced in him the idea that he couldn't treat players the same. The in-your-face speech he had given a slumping Beckham probably wouldn't work with a Quentin or a Konerko.

But he would talk with them. Yes, he would most definitely talk.

If you're a player, escape from Guillen is futile. He chats with players every day about anything, everything, and nothing. About their families. About the economy. About crazy drivers. About reality shows.

Some major-league managers steer clear of their players. They don't want to have anything more than a professional relationship. The players have their clubhouse, a manager has his office, and everyone meets in the dugout.

In Casa Guillen, there are no walls. He played for veteran manager Bobby Cox in Atlanta and coached under another veteran, Jack McKeon, in Florida. When he was named the Sox manager in November 2003, he didn't know what his clubhouse would look like, but he knew how it would sound: loud, like the team's new leader. The same will be true with the Marlins.

"Bobby Cox is an old-school manager," he said. "He doesn't hang around the clubhouse. I'm different. I'm old school the way I treat my players. I'm not going to put up with any shit. I'm going to tell them what they should do. But I'm a new generation because I talk with my players. I'll have a drink with them. I'm motherfucking them to their face when they're not doing things right."

Guillen walks through the clubhouse often, and very little gets by him. The distraught rookie. The resentful veteran who believes the manager is unfairly depriving him of at-bats. The pitcher who believes the manager shouldn't have pulled him in the fifth inning.

All different. All in need of talking to.

"Managing is like fishing," he said. "You put a hook on your line, you catch the fish, you let him go. You do it again. Back and forth, back and forth. That's what it is. You let the players play. When they don't do the things they should be doing, you call them back and tell them. Then you let them go to play again. That's the way you deal with the players."

Vizquel wants to be a manager some day. He spent the 2010 and 2011 seasons, his twenty-second and twenty-third in the big leagues, with the White Sox, and he spent a lot of time watching how Guillen does his job. If he's lucky enough or cursed enough to become a manager, he'll take from Guillen something besides hit-and-run strategies and small-ball philosophy.

"I'll take his attitude," Vizquel said. "His attitude is great. Approach the game with the same happiness that he approaches it with every day. You can see a smile on his face. He's the guy who guides this team, and if you can see the manager like that, it brings you a good vibe. And I think it's contagious."

That energy and that vibe can be tiring for the people around Ozzie. White Sox players will get a nice change of pace with his replacement, Robin Ventura, a mellower fellow. The Marlins will embrace Guillen, who is livelier than the man he replaced, the eighty-year-old McKeon. That's how it works in sports. The new guy is always a breath of fresh air. For a while.

Guillen takes a scattershot approach to life. Keep talking, keep reaching out to your players, and at least you'll have their attention. And getting attention is the whole idea, right?

Not everyone listens.

It was no secret that Guillen didn't get along with former Sox reliever Damaso Marte, a pitcher from the Dominican Republic who never seemed to be able to reach the heights his talent suggested he should. In 2005, the year the White Sox won the World Series, Marte showed up late before a game with the Angels. Earlier in the season, Guillen had been upset that Marte had hidden an arm injury, revealing it only after he had pitched poorly.

And now late for a game? It was clear to Guillen that the left-hander didn't deserve to be treated like a veteran. He deserved to be treated like a defiant child. Guillen told him to go home. The two men got into a shouting match.

"You don't like me!" Marte screamed. Guillen didn't disagree.

The situation festered. Guillen let Marte sit at home while the team played in Kansas City.

He set aside his distaste for Marte when he put the reliever's return in the hands of the players. They would have the final vote on whether he stayed or went. But Guillen did have an opinion.

"We need this guy to win," he told them.

The players voted to allow Marte back on the team. Though he was still deep in Guillen's doghouse, he emerged long enough to win Game 3 of the World Series, a fourteen-inning marathon against the Houston Astros.

The Sox traded him to Pittsburgh after the season.

Lesson?

"You're not going to be loved by everyone, but you're going to be loved by a lot of people," Guillen said. "I tell my players, 'I don't care if you love me or you fucking hate me because at one point in the season I'm going to hate you, too. Just respect me because I will respect you back.' "

It's simplistic to say that, in terms of management style, Ozzie Guillen is leading a discussion group while Tony La Russa was engaged in a chess match. Obviously, over a thirty-three-year career, La Russa got his players to play for him. If he hadn't, he wouldn't have won more than 2,700 games and three World Series in the big leagues before retiring after winning it all with the St. Louis Cardinals in 2011. And if Guillen were all thumbs as a strategist, he wouldn't have more victories than losses, nor would he have a World Series title and a Manager of the Year award on his résumé. The Marlins wouldn't have chased him so hard.

But the images the two managers project couldn't be more different.

The dugout is where Guillen holds court with the media before most games. He is not in the least like La Russa, who took himself Very Seriously. When media members gathered around La Russa, it was clear they felt a duty to ask the perfect question so as not to offend his baseball sensibilities. With Guillen, reporters can ask anything, and he will say anything.

You can ask Guillen about the flashy way Vizquel dresses.

"He's the worst dresser in baseball," he said. "Very expensive but very bad."

And Vizquel takes it. Gladly.

"He talks to everybody just like he's another player," Vizquel said. "I think that's the way that you have to communicate with your players and push the right buttons for everybody. Not everybody's the same way."

The reality in pro sports is that the athletes, not the coaches or managers, run the show. This is based on the relative size of contracts and on star power. A standout baseball player typically makes millions of dollars a year more than his manager. Fans fill the seats hoping to see the power hitter slug home runs. They don't come to see the manager inform the umpire of a lineup change.

This is where it gets tricky with Guillen. He loves the spotlight, and the spotlight loves him back. So how to balance that neediness with the responsibility of seeing to the needs of twenty-five different personalities? Guillen's definition of a good manager has nothing to do with in-game decisions. In his mind, a good manager should think of himself as a servant. If he's right, it would make him the most quoted servant in history.

"The most important thing is that players believe you and trust you," he said. "They know that when you say something, you mean it, good or bad. They know you are here for them. They're not here for you. That's important. A lot of managers and coaches think the players are there for them. No, we're here for them. We are the players' employees. We work for them.

"You have to be honest. You have to tell the truth to them. Be open. They have to know that they don't have a manager or a coach next to you—they have a friend. Even if you don't like me, you have a friend. We all have problems, and I can try to resolve your problem the best I can.

"Through the years, sometimes I've gotten my heart broken because stuff happens. But in the meanwhile, I don't regret it because I know what I did was best for the players. I think about them."

Bobby Jenks is one of the players who has taken a mallet to Guillen's heart. He had been an unlikely contributor to the Sox' 2005 World Series championship, a hard-throwing rookie whose off-field issues had chased him out of the Anaheim Angels' minor-league system. When he arrived at the Angels' spring-training facility in 2001, he had burns on his hands and arms. According to a 2003 story in *ESPN The Magazine*, he had scorched himself "in a drunken stupor," using a lighter to open a wound the size of a silver dollar on his right hand—his pitching hand. He burned his left hand, too, then both forearms. And then he passed out. Jenks told the Angels he burned himself lifting the engine out of his car. He hadn't realized it was hot, he said.

In 2002, the Angels suspended him for sneaking beer onto the team bus, then demoted him from Double-A to Single-A.

Arm troubles dogged him, and the Angels finally waived him in December 2004. When the White Sox claimed him for $20,000, his career was on life support. He was twenty-three.

It was this fragile ballplayer who came to Chicago in the summer of 2005 after thirty-five games with the Birmingham Barons, the Sox' Double-A affiliate. There was no denying his talent. His fastball had been known to hit 100 mph, with movement on it, making him unhittable at times. There was still a lot of doubt about his personal life, however.

Guillen already had talked with him during spring training—like a friend, like a father, he said.

"You continue to do this, you're going to ruin your life," he told Jenks. "Whatever happened in the past is over. If you are not strong enough to turn this page in the past, you are not going to be strong enough to be a closer in the major leagues."

It finally clicked for Jenks. He was the closer by the time the playoffs arrived in 2005, and he saved five games in the postseason. He was an All-Star the next two seasons, racking up a combined eighty-one saves. But he struggled toward the end of his stay in Chicago, and his conditioning seemed to be a never-ending issue with Guillen. The White Sox decided not to re-sign him after the 2010 season, and he signed as a free agent with the Boston Red Sox.

Guillen believed he had treated Jenks well, had sat the kid down and shown him that he cared about him as a human being. Then again, it's a lot easier to show concern about someone who throws 100 mph than it is to show concern about a junk-ball pitcher. But the fact is that the White Sox had taken a chance on Jenks when other teams refused to touch him with a ten-foot fungo bat.

And they had helped him grow from a troubled, immature twenty-three-year-old into a major-league closer. Guillen knew he couldn't treat Jenks like anybody else. The kid had arrived in Chicago with unique issues. There had to be firmness to go with the pats on the back.

Just as Guillen has learned it's impossible to treat every player the same, he has learned every player won't treat him the same. This is what Jenks told MLB.com in December 2010, after signing with the Red Sox: "I want to play for a manager who trusts his relievers, regardless of what's going on. With the way Ozzie was talking this winter and the way he treated me, I don't want to fight with the guy. How many times did he question my ability and then say how he would love to have me back, but I would have to come to spring training and fight for the closer's role like anyone else?

"Why would I come back to that negativity? I'm looking forward to playing for a manager [Terry Francona] who knows how to run a bullpen."

Long after Oney Guillen's return fire about Jenks had joined the space debris of the social-media universe, Ozzie still felt betrayed.

Most people, in or out of baseball, don't operate the way Guillen does. Most people don't want confrontation. If they have an issue, they're more likely to complain to someone else than take it up with the guilty party.

Guillen believes the rest of the world should be like him. If he's upset with a player, he tells him to his face. Then he'll oftentimes tell the media what he told the player. Jenks skipped a step and went right to the media. It stung Guillen. That's one of the contradictions about him: his tongue is sharp, but he bleeds easily.

"I give a lot of myself to the players and they turn around

to say stuff about me: 'I didn't like this. I didn't like that,'" he said. "You know what? You had your opportunity to tell me about it when you were here with me. Why didn't you say it? If I have something to say to you, I will call you to my office and say, 'Hey, I don't like this.' Or ask how we can work to make this thing better. But sometimes it's like, wow, did we really treat these guys bad? They don't know what they have here until they leave. When they leave, they say, 'Shoot, it was pretty good there.'"

Every player is different. But every perceived betrayal cuts the same.

"Players know I love them," Guillen said. "They know. They know I care about them. Players know I'm going to be mad at them. Why? Because I'm a human being. Because I should be mad. I should be happy. One thing about it, I never get mad about a bad pitch. I'm never mad at an error. I get mad at bad execution. I get mad if I see something I don't like. I tell them, 'If you have any feeling about me, something in the back of your mind, you want me to know about it, I'm here. Whatever you see, whatever you hear, this is what I am.' It's easier for them to know who I am than for me to know everyone. I have to know twenty, thirty people. They know one guy."

The one guy likes to sit in his clubhouse office, the incense wafting out his open door. People walk in and out. When traffic slows to a halt, he gets up and goes looking for conversation. Sometimes the conversation comes looking for him. Sometimes it's a conversation he'd prefer not having.

At the end of July 2011, the Sox were part of a three-team trade that sent the utility infielder Mark Teahen to Toronto and the starting pitcher Edwin Jackson to the St. Louis Cardinals, via the Blue Jays. After the trade, Guillen looked as if he had lost a brother or two. He woke up that morning with a sick feeling in his stomach, knowing he was going to have to say good-bye. He's not good at good-byes.

"My job is not hard when I talk to the media, when fans talk, when I lose a game," he said. "The hardest part of my job is when we trade players, when we release players. That's the hardest thing for me to handle. Everything else to me comes with the game. When you're in love with the players, when you get along with the players very well, to tell them bye and good luck, that's one thing I hate about this job. Sometimes you think twice about being close to the players, but I can't change."

Baseball fans give managers too much of the credit and too much of the blame. In most games, managers have the least amount of control of anyone in uniform. They can't hit. They can't pitch. They can't run or field. Even when they make a decision, the success of that decision depends on the pitchers who pitch, the hitters who hit, or the base runners who run.

You can see how a manager might fall into utter hopelessness. He wants to grab a game by its pinstripes and shake it. But it's up to the players to do that. The only real control he has is in the pencil he holds when he fills out the lineup card. He decides who plays and who doesn't.

And that doesn't always carry negative connotations. That pencil can be a friend to a struggling player like Adam Dunn. Throughout the 2011 season, as Dunn's problems at the plate continued, Guillen looked to give him shelter from the storm.

"You can protect him from pitchers with a couple days off, let him clear his mind," he said. "Besides that, let them play. Make sure those guys know you're behind them for real. Make sure they know that no matter what happens, you're going to be there for them. Because at the end of the day, the players are going to be here. I'm the one that's going to get fired. Well, I want to get fired my way. My way is, let those guys play and resolve their own problems."

Fired? Who said anything about getting fired? Ozzie did, over and over again.

·2·

PROTECT YOUR EMPLOYEES FROM THE BARBARIANS

Ozzie Guillen's modus operandi is as obvious as Day-Glo: Take all the negative attention off a struggling player or a struggling team and put it on himself. Let him rise up to all of his five-foot-eleven frame and absorb the blame. *Please* let him. He lives for it. There is something at once generous and comical about the way he jumps on grenade after grenade for his players. The man collects shrapnel like some kids collect baseball cards. He wouldn't trade it for the world.

"Give me the pressure," he said. "I'll take the pressure. I take thc heat. Let the guys play. Let my players play. Anything that's negative, I take it. I want to take all the heat. I want to take all the pressure myself, and hopefully I can handle it."

Ozzie Guillen, human shield.

After losing a game to the Toronto Blue Jays in 2008, his team's sixth straight loss, Mount Guillen erupted in front of the media. It was a calculated explosion, meant to take the pressure off his players and to inform them that when God divvied up the sides, He decided it would be the White Sox against the world.

Amid all the sarcasm in his outburst, Guillen somehow managed to weave in his distaste for the Cubs' hold on the city of Chicago. That's called "multitasking," class.

"We won [the World Series] a couple years ago, and we're horseshit," he told reporters. "The Cubs haven't won in 120 years, and they're the fucking best. Fuck it, we're good. Fuck everybody. We're horseshit, and we're going to be horseshit the rest of our lives, no matter how many World Series we win. We are the bitch of Chicago. We're the Chicago bitch. We have the worst owner—the guy's got seven fucking rings, and he's the fucking horseshit owner."

The White Sox went on to win twelve of their next seventeen games.

"There's a method to his madness," said White Sox pitcher John Danks. "Whenever we need the attention taken off us or if he needs to do something to loosen us up, I think Ozzie knows what he's doing. Ozzie's a character, no doubt, but there have been times when he's said things or done things where it's almost planned."

Are his efforts meant to protect the players or to bring attention to the manager? It's the debate about Guillen that won't go away. What's not up for debate is whether he likes it or not. Managers forever have tried to take pressure off their teams by deflecting criticism that might otherwise barrel into their players. Few have enjoyed doing it as much as Guillen has.

So, heat? Oh, goodness, bring it on. Heat will never get a warmer reception than the one Guillen will give it. He talks almost giddily about the heat. Heat is a respected opponent. It has flesh and bones, body and soul, and it and him are in a cage match. A huge crowd is watching, which is part of the allure.

"Pressure?" he said. "Never. Never. Never. You know what's pressure to me? My dad. He's broke down in Venezuela, waiting for me to send the paycheck every fifteen days. That's pressure.

"Me? I'm fine. I love the heat. I love the heat. I don't hide from anybody. I like to be in the hot seat. If they don't play good, I should be fired. If they play good, they should keep me. That's the way it is.

"I never feel pressured by any circumstances. Never. Never. In my life, when I was a kid. Now that I'm a grown man, I know what I can do. I have a lot of confidence in myself, a lot of confidence in my coaching staff. That's the reason they spent a lot of money on this ball club and give it to me—because they have confidence in me.

"They can fire me and give the ball club to somebody else. No. I'm very comfortable where I am right now. Very comfortable."

Those thoughts came hours before the White Sox' 2011 season opener in Cleveland, which would seem like an odd time to be talking about job termination. But when you walk with Ozzie, all roads lead to this topic. It's his favorite mode of deflection, though he would never admit it. Several times a month in each baseball season, he brings it up unbidden. Even in 2005, when he won a World Series, he talked about going to live on his boat near his off-season Miami home if Reinsdorf decided that he, Guillen, was no longer capable of doing the job.

There are certain givens in life. Death. Taxes. The sun setting in the west. And Ozzie Guillen at some point saying the owner should fire him if the team is doing poorly. This will happen with the Marlins, too. The only question is how soon.

It is his tried-and-true way of protecting his players in tough times, but it also comes from his need to take responsibility. It's something he had decided on as a fourteen-year-old who was all but living on his own in Venezuela. He would try not to blame anybody else for his own failures. He would carry any burden presented to him, in addition to the one already on his back. It's why he took responsibility over and over for the White Sox' poor season in 2011.

Whenever Guillen talks about getting fired, it tends to suck up all other discussion, the way a black hole sucks in everything around it. It came in handy a little more than a month into the 2011 season, when the Sox were bad. Not just standard-issue bad, but bad beyond belief. Exquisitely bad. Cover-your-eyes bad. They had the worst record in baseball.

But this time, the subject of his getting fired was not just another arrow in his quiver of motivational tools. The calls for his head were loud and getting louder. They were on radio sports talk shows. They were on Internet discussion boards. Guillen heard them and read all about them, even though he claims he ignores media reports about his team.

On May 7, baseball writer Phil Rogers of the *Chicago Tribune* led off a column with the reasonable assessment that firing Guillen wasn't going to solve the Sox' problems. But while Rogers was at it, he listed sixteen possible replacements if the team canned its manager. That's the climate Guillen found himself in. Few people in Chicago believed Reinsdorf was going to send Ozzie to the managers' graveyard, but no one seemed averse to kicking the tires on a hearse, just in case. The temptation was to describe all the losing as a Greek tragedy, but nobody had died and a Trojan horse filled with .300 hitters hadn't arrived. Help was not on the way.

So now Guillen was rummaging through his bag of tricks to rejuvenate his team, to kick some ass, to get the critics off his players' backs, to divert attention from a club that was shockingly awful. He went where he always goes, to his thoughts of being fired.

"At this point, I don't trust anyone," he said of his job status. "Do you think Jerry is going to come to me and say, 'Listen, we might fire you'? What do you think I'm going to say? No? Hey, man, you've got a lot of reasons to do it. How many games have we lost? Twenty games already? You have 120 million reasons [dollars] and you have thirty reasons [players and coaches] about why we're not winning. You think I'm going to tell Jerry don't do it? No."

The night before, he had watched his team hit rock bottom, which wasn't as bad as it sounds. At least it had hit something. Minnesota Twins pitcher Francisco Liriano had come into the Sox' offense-friendly ballpark and thrown a no-hitter, despite the fact he had brought with him a 1–4 record and a fleshy 9.13 earned-run average. It wasn't as if Liriano had been sharp that night. He had walked six batters.

But the White Sox, who had entered the season believing they were going to be contenders for the American League Central title, couldn't have hit a metal baseball if they were swinging magnetic bats. Their $127 million payroll, fifth highest in Major League Baseball, had raised huge expectations on the South Side of Chicago, and perhaps the Sox were feeling the full weight of those hopes and those dreams and those dollars.

Everyone had been expecting Guillen to erupt. They had been looking for signs of seismic activity. There had been a few rumbles but nothing large. He said privately that an eruption was the last thing his players needed at that moment. To send up fire and ashes so early in the season would be a sign he was panicking. And if he panicked, he believed, his players would follow suit.

The players, on the other hand, were ready for anything from their leader.

"With Ozzie . . . it's kind of like the Tasmanian devil, where you don't know," said middle reliever Will Ohman. "His reactions sometimes are unexpected. But you know what you're going to get. You don't know when you're going to get it, but you know what you're going to get."

The "when" arrived near the end of May. Guillen might have believed with all his heart that this was a time for him to act presidential and not like a general leading an amateurish coup. But, well, all the losing was beyond his ability to control himself.

The eruption was vintage Ozzie, full of volcanic debris, misunderstandings, misinterpretations, and general confusion. It was sound and fury signifying *something*, though afterward witnesses would huddle together to try to make sense of what that something was.

It came after a fourteen-inning loss in Toronto on May 28 and carried over into the next day like a stalled weather system. Guillen cleared his throat. It was like a maestro picking up his baton. The tongue unfurled. He ripped the team. The next day, he seemed to rip the fans. Then he ripped the media for saying he had ripped the fans.

What set him off initially was his team's failure to take advantage of scoring opportunities in the game, especially in the late innings. He had done his best La Russa imitation, trying to create something out of nothing strategically. He had used Gavin Floyd, a starter, in relief. He had put Omar Vizquel at first base for the first time in the infielder's long career.

That improvisation had earned him some criticism. Ozzie played Vizquel *where?* Why was young reliever Chris Sale allowed to stay in the game for a career-high three innings?

As is often the case with Ozzie, no one was exactly sure where he had heard the criticism. Sometimes he gets bits of information from friends and family who read the papers or listen to the talk shows. Other times, he expands one fan's unhappiness into general public dissatisfaction. A few tweets turn into what he perceives as a flock of abuse. There is criticism he sees and some he imagines. He insists it doesn't bother him when someone questions his baseball acumen.

This time, it really didn't matter where the criticism had originated. What mattered was that it had reached Guillen in Toronto after that fourteen-inning loss to the Blue Jays. The spark had grown up to be a forest fire.

The next day, he talked with reporters about the thankless job coaches have. He talked about a general lack of appreciation for coaches. He said his life would be so much easier and so much less stressful if he didn't care so much for the White Sox organization. And, of course, he used the F word. No, no that one. This one: *Fired.*

"People only care when you lose games: 'He should get fired,'" he said. "When we win games, they say, 'Those guys are great players.'"

If this was Calculating Ozzie, he was doing a great job of acting. It more likely was Hurt Ozzie. It's one of the contradictions about him. He gladly takes the abuse in order to protect his players, but he's still stung by that abuse. In his lengthy discussion with the media, he envisioned what it would be like for the organization to honor him, the coaching staff, and the players before a game many seasons in the future.

"Are they going to feel sorry because we're going to get fired? Fuck no," he said. "They only remember us from 2005. In 2020, we'll come here in a wheelchair all fucked up. As soon as you leave the ballpark, they don't care about you anymore. They don't. The monuments, the statue they got, they pee on it when they're drunk. That's all they do. Thank you for coming, bye-bye. Thank you for coming for thirty minutes for all the suffering you did all your life, day in and day out."

This is where the parsing started. Who was this "they" to whom Ozzie referred? It seemed to be White Sox fans. Who else gets drunk at baseball games? Certainly not the media, though Guillen might argue it would improve the writing and reporting ability of many a reporter.

When his words showed up in news stories online, he became incensed that some reporters had interpreted them as a slam on the fans. He claimed he meant that critics in the media, not Sox fans, would piss on players' and managers' statues.

He fully understood what it would look like if he were ripping the fans who buy the tickets. He had always held himself up as a man of the people, a person willing to speak his mind like every other hardworking guy on the South Side of Chicago. It is part of his charm. He had completely bought into Sox fans' caricature of Cubs fans as being less interested in baseball than in partying at Wrigley Field.

So for him to take a swipe at Sox fans for being ungrateful would have been harmful to the reputation he had built for himself. He started tweeting like mad.

"They should print everything I said . . . that was low blow and irresponsible . . . no class . . . Bunch a crap . . . No mention any fans and alcohol."

The Sox issued a statement that sounded more like George Will's bow tie talking than Ozzie Guillen's lips: "If anyone listens to the entire conversation or reads a transcript of what I said, they will see my comments were not directed as criticism of White Sox fans."

The result of all the turmoil? There was zero attention on the players and the losing. Oh, and the White Sox went to Boston and swept the Red Sox. The team seemed to feed off Guillen's emotions, which, bottom line, is the whole point. Take the attention away from the flailing team. Throw your body on the incendiary device. Never mind that you're the one who threw the bomb in the first place. By the time it's over, no one will remember that detail.

"I'm getting criticized every day in my life," Guillen said. "People say, 'What the fuck are you doing? Why don't you hit and run, why don't you bunt?' That's my life. That's why this motherfucking thing [slapping himself on the back] is very strong. I've been criticized all my life. I don't give a fuck. I'm strong. I face the media with my head up."

But why does he put himself through it? Why not try to ignore the tweets, the newspaper columns, the talk shows?

"I don't give a shit," he said. "I really don't care. Those guys out there that are motherfucking me? I was a great manager for eight fucking innings earlier in the season. All of a sudden a guy drops a ball and we give up a run and I'm a piece of shit.

"To be honest with you, I'd rather have the fans be in my ass and criticize me. I want the fans and the media to criticize me and stay away from my players. If you want to know something about my players, I'll be honest. When the media and the fans get on the players because your manager's not honest, the media knows it's bullshit. I learned that as a player.

"I'd rather say, 'This is the way it is. I'll take the blame.' I'm the one who made the decision. I'm the one who thought this is going to be good for the team. This guy failed? Blame me because I'm the one who made that move."

It takes a certain kind of person to absorb abuse, to want to absorb it, to actually seek it out for the purpose of staging a head-on collision. The Toronto blowup was mostly Guillen's creation, helped along by what he called a misinformed media.

What kind of person puts himself through this?

"Deep down I think he likes it," A. J. Pierzynski said. "I don't know if he'd ever admit that. You'd have to like it a little bit, otherwise you wouldn't do it. He loves the attention. He's had a great career because of it. He brings focus to the White Sox and focus to the South Side, and it's not a bad thing all the time. I think he does a good job with when to do it and when not to do it."

Dan Gladden, the Twins radio analyst and a former Minnesota player, would later go on WSCR radio in Chicago and cut to the heart of the debate about Guillen in the baseball world.

"What Ozzie does well is he deflects the criticism from the players, and I think every good manager does that," Gladden said. "That's why he'll have those outbursts and some embarrassing moments at times. He's deflecting the criticism from the players, and it's on him. But at the same time, it's almost like enough is enough. It gets old. We've heard this, we've seen this before. Keeping guys loose in the clubhouse . . . let the players dictate and decide what kind of a clubhouse they want. It shouldn't be decided by the manager. He's won a World Series—you can't take that away from him—but I think it'd be distracting as a player."

Several days later, sitting in the dugout before a game, Ozzie feigned ignorance.

"Who's Dan Gladden?" he said. "Who's that? If that shit came from [Hall of Famer and Twins broadcaster] Bert Blyleven, I'd say, 'Wow. Shit.' But Dan Gladden? That's a pimple on my ass."

Kenny Williams walked into a coaches' meeting in the last week of June 2011 and said it was time to bring up the kid.

The kid was twenty-two-year-old Dayan Viciedo, a Cuban who was tearing it up for the White Sox' Triple-A affiliate in Charlotte. The big-league team needed offense.

"Okay, who are we going to sit?" Guillen said.

"Juan Pierre," Williams said.

A shouting match commenced between the general manager and the coaching staff. Guillen suggested that if Williams wanted to get rid of Pierre, a twelve-year major-league veteran, the general manager would have to be the one to inform the other twenty-four players of the move and deal with the ensuing uprising.

Pierre hadn't been doing what a traditional leadoff hitter is supposed to do: get on base often and, once on, be a baserunning threat. But Guillen loved Pierre as a player, perhaps more than he had loved any other player in his eight years of managing. Pierre arrived early for extra work. Three times a week, when pitchers and catchers practiced pickoffs and worked on throwing out base stealers, he worked on his leads.

He also practiced bunting and took extra fly balls in the outfield.

In other words, he was a manager's dream. Beyond that, other players looked up to him. He was a pro's pro. If he went 0-for-4, he acted no differently than if he had gone 4-for-4. He had a calming influence on players who tended to react unevenly to the ups and downs of a baseball season.

Guillen was concerned that if he benched Pierre, beyond insulting the player, the ties between him and his players would become frayed. In his eyes, demoting Pierre was a nonsubject, a nonstarter, nonsense.

"I might lose some respect from the players," he said. "People believe in him. They know he's our leader. I'm not afraid to bench a guy that's not producing, as long as I have something else better or equal. But I think he plays the game right. He works. A lot of people look up to him. Our players love him.

"I always say it's about winning. I don't care about feelings. But you have to be careful. You have to be careful how you treat your players, how your players are going to respond. If I do that to Juan, well, I never did it to anybody else. A lot of people have struggled, and I say, 'I'm not going to bench you.' I did give people a day off.

"Managing now is not about how good you are at strategy. It's how good you are with your players. The only way you can get the best out of the players is to show some respect."

Guillen countered with his own personnel suggestion, and it didn't go over well with Williams: bench Alex Rios, a high-priced, underperforming outfielder. It was a slap at Williams, who had picked up Rios on waivers in 2009 and absorbed much of his nearly $70 million contract. Rios was currently hitting .220.

Williams walked out of the meeting. Later, he made it clear to reporters why Viciedo had not been promoted to the majors, a move many White Sox fans wanted to see made.

"Ozzie is not ready to change the mix he has right now, and that has to be respected," Williams said, sounding like a recent graduate of diplomacy school.

So the burden was on Guillen, and he was more than happy to carry it. Was it coincidence that, a few days later, Guillen pulled Rios from a game for not running hard on the base paths? Statement made: He would always reward the player who worked hard.

"It's not the first time it happened," Guillen said. "I don't like the way he runs the bases. . . . And that's a message for everyone. If they don't fucking run the bases, their reputation comes on me, and I have a greater reputation in this fucking game to do it that way. They don't run the bases, they're out of the game. I don't give a shit if it's Paul Konerko or Adam Dunn or anyone. You don't run the bases, you're out of the game."

Pierre would win two straight games at the end of the month with key hits, including a two-run triple against the Cubs at Wrigley Field. Guillen would protect Pierre, at almost any cost, even if he went "0-for-100 in the next twenty games," he said after the victory over the Cubs.

Williams met with Guillen and the coaches the morning after Pierre's big game against the Cubs. There was no talk of Viciedo.

"I don't think he'll mention that after he saw Juan Pierre the last couple of games," Guillen said with a wry smile on his face.

In his mind, there was too much at stake.

"I don't play somebody because he's my friend," he said. "If I don't think that guy's the right guy for the team that particular day, I guarantee you I won't play him. I don't care what people are going to say. I think Juan is the type of player where you have to be careful what you do because all of a sudden a lot of people are going to look at you like, 'Wow, if you did it to Juan, you might do it to us.' You create that wall between players, coaches, and managers."

In the meantime, before Joey Cora called Dayan Viciedo that same night to check in, Guillen had a request: Make sure the kid knows I don't hate him. There's just no room here now.

Another of the contradictions about Guillen is that, as protective as he is of his players, he's not afraid to criticize them publicly or "throw them under the bus," the cliché he often uses.

He sees it as honesty. If he lies about a player's performance, he believes, it destroys his own credibility.

If a player fails to hustle or "doesn't play the game right," Guillen lets him know. Then the manager often goes to the media and offers up the same criticism he gave to the player in private. The vast majority of managers and coaches in professional sports are reluctant to call out an athlete publicly for a poor performance. Their preference is to keep it in-house to save the player embarrassment. For today's ballplayer, about the only thing worse than being embarrassed is coming up achingly short of a contract bonus. But it's about more than shielding players from public shame. Managers don't want their players pointing fingers at one another for fear it will lead to a divided clubhouse. They are deathly afraid of rifts. If a manager begins pointing a finger, it can lead to total chaos, or so the thinking goes.

Ozzie tilts his head and sees the world differently. The

fallout from *not* telling the truth is much worse than the possibility of a player's feelings getting hurt. If he lies, everything he says is open to question. And then where would he be?

It's an attitude that would be viewed with complete mistrust in the National Football League, where lying is part of the game. Teams fib about strategy, injuries, personnel decisions, and contract details. Coaches cover for players who blow assignments on the field and get arrested off it. Everything is cloaked in secrecy. Guillen would be considered a cancer in the NFL, a free radical spreading sedition, communism, and Lord knows what else.

More baseball managers lean in the direction of the NFL's attitude toward the truth than in Ozzie's direction. Most shy away from telling the media their innermost thoughts about the shortstop who failed to run hard to first on a groundout, believing it would ruin a relationship. When it comes to telling the truth, there's nothing in it for them.

Guillen sees it exactly the opposite: there's everything in it. There are no surprises when he tells the truth. The player knows where he stands with his manager. He knows that if he doesn't run out a ground ball, he and everybody else are going to hear about it. And the manager can stand in front of the media, and by extension the fans, and feel at peace for saying what everybody else is thinking anyway.

"As long as they play hard, I'll take the heat for them," he said. "Give me some bullets. But if I see a fucking guy not hustling and we're playing like shit, oh, fuck you, motherfucker. Then I'm on your ass.

"I take the heat. This is my job. I protect my players with anything I can as long as they do their shit right. I'll get fired for that shit."

He pulled Rios for not running the bases hard in a game against the Colorado Rockies. Then he explained to the media afterward how a lack of effort reflects poorly on the manager and the rest of the team. Rios could run lackadaisically, but he couldn't hide. It was on sports websites that night.

"Listen, bro," he told Rios, "I never criticize you because you're 0-for-4. I never criticize you missing balls. But I will get on your fucking ass if you don't respect the game."

In Guillen's mind, the worst thing that can happen to a manager is to lose the respect of his players. The easiest way for that to happen, he believes, is be dishonest. Again, it's backward compared with the approach taken by most other managers, who believe that publicly pointing out a player's shortcomings in a game is to risk insulting the player and thus to risk alienating him. They would prefer to alienate the media. Lose the clubhouse and you're going to lose your job, according to conventional wisdom.

Guillen is an equal-opportunity criticizer. Every player who doesn't play the game right is in his crosshairs and a candidate to get singled out in a press gathering. It doesn't matter who you are, from the highest-paid veteran to a September call-up. All are liable to feel Ozzie's dramatic interpretation of the truth.

Why does he do this? There's no other explanation than he can't help himself. There's right, and there's wrong. When Will Ohman pitched poorly early in the season, Guillen let him and everybody else know about it. Ohman should "get his head out of his ass," the manager told reporters.

"He was right," Ohman said later.

The approach is not always popular among the players, even the ones who like Guillen and can take his criticism.

"We know when we screw up as players," Pierzynski said. "People don't need to tell us that we screwed up. We know it. We have pride. We're competitive. We want to win, and we want to get a hit every time. We want to make every play and make every pitch. I will give Ozzie credit. Most of the time that he's said something to the media, he's already said something to you, so you already know it's coming. You still don't like to read it. But you know it's part of the game, and you know it's part of what you signed up for with the White Sox."

Now it's a package deal in Miami. When you sign a contract with the Marlins, you get the money and you get Ozzie, all of him—the encouragement, the outrageousness, the outbursts, the criticism, the loyalty, the fun, and enough noise to make you contemplate joining a monastery for the quiet.

Pierzynski complained several times to Guillen about the manager's habit of criticizing players publicly.

"He's said stuff in the newspaper," he said. "I've been like, 'Hey, man. Why? You don't need to say that stuff.' We sit down and we hash it out and get over it. One thing good about him is that once it's over, it's over. But more than once I've gone in there and said you don't need to say this stuff about me or somebody else. They know. We talk about it and move on."

Pierzynski found himself under the bus and with tire tracks across his chest in 2011. In a June game, the Twins had stolen five bases with Gavin Floyd on the mound and Pierzynski behind the plate. Pierzynski doesn't throw out many runners anyway, but in his comments to the media after the game, he had alluded to Floyd's reputation for being easy to steal on. At that point in the season, base runners were 15-for-15 in steal attempts with the right-hander on the mound.

Guillen believed Pierzynski needed to take some of the

blame. Floyd had gone to a slide step in order to speed up his delivery and give base runners less time to steal. At that point, the catcher had thrown out only seven of forty-one base runners.

Ozzie revved the bus's engine and shifted into gear after Pierzynski's comments about Floyd.

"A guy steals second and third with a slide step, you have to wear it," he said of Pierzynski. "You gotta admit you're not throwing the ball well right now. That's why we continue to work twice a week trying to get pitchers to go to the plate more quickly. If you have to take the blame, take the blame.

"The people think it's your fault, it's somebody's fault. It's not my fault. It has to be between the pitcher and catcher, and the pitcher went slide step twice.

"When the team loses, I take the heat. When they steal bases, obviously A. J.'s gotta wear it and live with it."

When it comes to taking the blame for losses, Guillen is almost always the first in line. That's where he draws the line on his public criticism. He'll rip someone for not playing the game right, but he won't hang a loss on a player in public.

It's a nuance that sometimes is lost on his players. Most would prefer he talk broadly about the team with the media, rather than critique individual performances when those performances are below par.

But to Guillen, it all comes back to honesty. In mid-April, some fans sitting behind the Sox dugout at the Cell, as the ballpark is called, began screaming about the reliever Matt Thornton, who was supposed to be the closer but had looked more like a casino greeter for opposing batters.

Ozzie turned to the fans and screamed back.

"Would you relax? Just relax! We're only ten games into the season!"

A day later, after Thornton had blown a lead in the ninth inning and then lost the game in the tenth, Guillen declared at his postgame press conference, "We have no closer."

It is true he's every bit as mercurial as those fans were. It's also true he'd be a perfect radio talk-show host, happily allowing his emotions to be yanked back and forth by the events of the day. But his comments about the closer situation were ruthlessly accurate. At that point, the Sox didn't have a closer, despite the fact they had given Thornton a two-year, $12 million contract extension before the season. The hell if Guillen was going to stand in front of the media, and the fans, and say otherwise.

He periodically has to remind his players why he's so honest with the media. Many of them don't understand how much he has to deal with reporters. With the sheer volume of interview sessions and the sheer breadth of Ozzie's opinions, well, things are going to be said. And they're not always going to be popular. During a long season, a manager's frustration is bound to jump its banks. Guillen broke it down mathematically for the more sensitive members of his team.

"I told my players the other day, 'Listen, I talk to the media 162 games plus 31 preseason games. That's 193. I talk to them before and after the game. That's 386 times a season, and I'm motherfucking you four times? Okay, motherfucker, how many times did I protect your fucking ass? Four times I get the red ass? I'm a human being. You get to throw the helmet. You can kick everything. But I can't get the ass? Why? Because I'm the manager? I'm a human being. I've got blood flowing through my veins. Fuck you, motherfucker.' "

Nothing riles up Ozzie more than perceived lack of effort. There are sins, there are cardinal sins, and then there is Playing the Game the Wrong Way.

"I never go off on the players about a play or a home run," he said. "But if they go out there and it seems like they don't care? Fuck you. Then I go to the media and let them know what's going on.

"Look at all the times I got the ass and why. They say 'Ozzie's crazy.' No, I tell you the way it is. We played in Tampa and we had the bases loaded like three times and we lose the game. I'm gonna be happy? Well, if you [players] are, I'm not. I don't say you're not trying.

"But we come in the clubhouse and a fucking basketball game's on TV. Okay, what do you want me to do? Laugh? You don't care about this shit? They eat and drink beer and watch the NBA. At least fake it!"

Near the end of July, the Sox lost 2–1 in eleven innings to the Kansas City Royals in the final game of a three-game series. It was galling because they couldn't find a way to hit Bruce Chen, who would never be mistaken for a flamethrower. But he had been blessed with great control, and he was especially effective on a hot, muggy night.

During the previous series in Detroit, Guillen had taken the same gentle path he had taken most of the season. He had talked about a Sox team that had heart, effort, talent—everything but a winning record. But he had been certain that even that last unfortunate detail would eventually be reversed.

Against the Royals, though, the Sox had wasted a wonderful effort by their starting pitcher John Danks and Guillen was irate about an absence of anything vaguely resembling fire. He was tired of protecting his team and tired of painting a rosy picture that only he seemed to be able to see.

And making matters worse, the Sox had lost to Chen, a left-hander who threw junk and used an assortment of delivery angles to fool hitters. Hitters walked away with the feeling reserved for people who suspect they've just been bilked in a shell game.

Could life get any worse? Yes, as a matter of fact, it could. In the eighth inning, a foul ball bounced off the netting behind home plate and caromed toward the Sox dugout, hitting Guillen below the right eye. There was a noticeable bump on his face after the game.

There was also noticeable steam coming out of his ears. His postgame press conference lasted all of one minute, thirty-one seconds, most of it in response to an innocent question about his face: "How are you feeling?" The tape was played in its entirety on ESPN's *SportsCenter* the next morning. The bleeps sounded like a traffic jam during rush hour.

"Nothing more painful than losing the fucking game against Bruce Chen once again. That's more painful than this one. Fucking pathetic. No fucking energy. We just go by the motions. We take the day off instead of tomorrow.

"If we go to Cleveland and play the way we did in Kansas City, it's going to be a fucking dead-ass July. That's very bad. Nothing against Bruce Chen, I have a lot of respect for this kid. But our approach at the plate, that's not a good club out there. Fuck it. I'm tired of protecting people and try to say what I say.

"I take my shit back, what I said in Detroit. I take it back. This thing is one day at a time. One day we're good, three days we're bad. We don't have energy in the dugout. Horseshit approach at the plate for the ninetieth time.

"Fuck. If we go to Cleveland the way we go here, good luck. We're wasting our money on this club if we go to Cleveland the way we were here. That's all we have to say.

"That's the team we have all year long. That's the club. [People say] I talk shit because I have to talk shit. No, I don't. I talk shit because what I see. That's all I see. Very bad. Nothing against Chen. Nothing against Kansas City's pitching staff. They're good. They got a young ball club. The way we go about our business here, horseshit. They can say whatever they want to say.

"If we go to Cleveland that way, and then we got to play New York, Boston, and Detroit, good luck."

The day after the Chen debacle, Guillen talked about the possibility of getting fired again, of going out his way, and so on. He was asked if it was possible his outburst might cause a schism in the clubhouse, where perhaps not everyone was happy to hear the manager going off about a lack of enthusiasm among players. Lack of enthusiasm is next-door neighbors with lack of effort.

"I get paid to win games, not to make friends," Guillen said. "It's my job, motivation. I have my own way to motivate people. When you're winning, you're a motivator. When you're losing, you're a loser. My job is to win games, and I'm not doing what I'm supposed to."

Guillen is sensitive to any talk that free agents don't want to play for him because of his reputation for stripped-down honesty. There's no real proof that that has been the case. No player has stepped forward to say he bypassed Chicago because the manager was publicly critical of players. And the Marlins landed former Mets star Jose Reyes and former White Sox pitcher Mark Buehrle after the 2011 season.

But free agents do ask Guillen's players about him. They want to know about Crazy Ozzie. Is it true that he thinks he, and not his team, is the show?

"The guys coming in here new, the first thing I tell them is, 'Don't believe what you hear,'" Guillen said. "The first question these guys ask our players is, 'How do you like playing for Ozzie?' I tell them, 'You will like it here. I don't bother these guys.'

"Sometimes we treat players better than we should. We respect. We love. I never say no to any of my players.

"People say, 'They don't want to play for Ozzie.' Well, if I'm so terrible, I have Konerko back. I have A. J. back. Konerko could have gone and made a lot of money somewhere else. You can go talk to Buehrle, Juan Uribe, whoever. The biggest satisfaction is when you see your former players and they hug you and they talk to you. That's all you can do."

Money talks the loudest in baseball, louder even than Guillen. Players generally take the most lucrative offer. Paul Konerko was no exception. He said his decision to choose the Sox over the Diamondbacks after the 2010 season had to do with contract offers, not sentimentality. The Sox offered him a three-year, $37.5 million deal to remain in Chicago. Arizona offered $30 million over the same span.

That's pretty simple math.

"I didn't want to come back just because I've been here," Konerko said. "That would've been a stupid reason."

Most of the players in the White Sox clubhouse would shrug when the topic of Guillen's sometimes brutal honesty came up. That's life, they said, the way breathing and eating and sleeping are life. Chicago is a difficult place to play. Success doesn't come around the city often, and when it does, it doesn't stay long. The Cubs' difficulties are notorious, and their fans, after decades of enabling the "Lovable Losers" by filling Wrigley Field despite the team's limited success, have become increasingly frustrated and angry.

White Sox fans, though with a World Series title in their recent past, are extremely demanding. An argument could be made that life with Ozzie helped toughen up players to deal with Chicago's sharp edges. If you could make it there, you could make it anywhere. Or was that phrase spoken for?

The Marlins might not get the media scrutiny the Sox do, but some of the Miami players are going to have to grow tougher skin nonetheless.

"Ozzie's preparing guys, in a sense," Will Ohman said. "As a player, you're dealing in the clubhouse with what you're going to see out there. He's a tough-love guy. There's no one person that's going to affect everybody the same way. There's not going to be one person that's going to be liked by everybody. Certain styles work for certain people. That's why you see managing changes a lot. But if you've risen to this level and you can't take the criticism, you're in the wrong business."

There are a lot of major-league ballplayers in the wrong business, then.

Things are cyclical with Guillen. There's emotion, reaction, and, every once in a while, regret. He blows up; he calms down; everybody moves on.

If you took every word that Ozzie has ever spoken and strung them together into one long run-on sentence, you could circumnavigate the globe several times and make a side trip to the moon. But if you ask him whether he regrets anything he has said to the media, he can come up with just one, and it had nothing to do with his team. That means he talks and rarely looks back.

In a 2006 *Sports Illustrated* story, Guillen questioned whether Yankees star Alex Rodriguez had truly considered playing for the Dominican Republic in the World Baseball Classic, as he had said, before deciding to play for the United States team. Rodriguez was born in New York, but his parents were from the Dominican Republic, giving him dual citizenship.

Guillen was skeptical of Rodriguez's sincerity, to say the least.

"He knew he wasn't going to play for the Dominicans," he told *Sports Illustrated*. "He's not a Dominican. I hate hypocrites. He's full of shit."

Not surprisingly, the response from Yankees owner George Steinbrenner favored the person wearing pinstripes.

"Shut it up," the Boss said. "I like Ozzie Guillen as a manager, but I don't like him when he pops off like that. That's bullshit."

Guillen apologized to Rodriguez, not because he didn't believe what he said to be the truth, but because it had caused another round of questions and, in some quarters, more condemnation for A-Rod.

Other than that, Guillen has a hard time coming up with any other instances of foot-in-mouth disease.

"Everybody else?" he said. "Check out who throws the first punch. It's not me. I've got to defend myself."

It's true that the bull is the one that charges, but the bullfighter has been known to shake his cape now and then.

"You ask me a question, I'm going to answer you," Guillen said. "I never go out of my way unless somebody asks me a question. I'm going to give you the most honest answer I can give in my heart and my brains. If people like it or don't like it, what the fuck should I do? I can sleep at night."

Most managers want their players on the same page, offering up the same bland gruel for public consumption. Nobody gets mad and nobody gets hurt. The peace is preserved and the team presumably plays better because of it. Everybody pulls in the same direction.

If that's the right way to do things, it would seem to follow that Guillen's approach would lead to anarchy. If the manager was given to outrageous statements and if honesty had been the currency of choice in the White Sox organization, it would make sense that the trickle-down effect would have led to friction among players, if not drawn-out wars. But that wasn't the case with the Sox, where conflict was kept to a minimum.

Jermaine Dye and Orlando Cabrera got into a scuffle in the dugout during a game in 2008. Cabrera was new to the team, but in his short time in Chicago he had earned a reputation as being a selfish ballplayer. In that game, he had stolen third base with Dye at the plate. Some hitters consider that a distraction. Words were exchanged, and players moved to restrain the two.

Ozzie's reaction to the shoving match?

"Everybody wanted to break it up," he said. "I said, 'Uh-uh, let [Dye] kick his ass. Let him fucking go get him.' Everybody was like, 'What?' I think J. D. was right, and he was tired of that shit."

Guillen isn't a hawk. He's not a dove, either. He's a whooping crane, which has a call that can be heard from three miles away.

"I protect the players more than any manager," he said. "I protect them for real. For real."

In other words, all the other stuff—his outbursts, his public critiques of the players, and so forth—doesn't matter in the end. What matters is that when the fans wanted the heads of Pierre and Dunn in 2011, Guillen was there to fight off the hordes. What matters is that Guillen is there when it matters. The rest is just words.

In late July, Sox fans were still blaming Ozzie for his hardheadedness when it came to the Pierre-Viciedo debate, but the truth was that Dunn and Rios—two people Guillen had been protecting as if they were priceless diamonds—had inadvertently turned Pierre into a piñata for the fan base. Their failure at the plate was to blame for the uproar about Viciedo.

Guillen finally stated that obvious truth. He didn't throw the two veterans under the bus, but he let everyone know what the reality was.

"If Dunn and Rios and all those guys swing the bat right now, maybe people don't even know what Viciedo looks like," he said. "They won't even know who he was, especially with that name. If those two guys were doing what they were supposed to do, they wouldn't know who that guy is. . . . Those guys aren't hitting, and that's why his name comes up. If we think Viciedo is going to be our solution, he can help. But he's not our solution. He's not."

Everyone is linked to everyone else on a baseball team. There were real repercussions to Dunn's and Rios's hitting woes, well beyond a lack of run production. If they didn't know that before, they knew it now.

It's hard to see how Guillen keeps track of all the deflecting he does. If he deflects the pressure off one guy, maybe he's putting it on somebody else. Or is he simply protecting himself, as some have said? That it always has been and always will be about him?

There's no doubt Guillen sometimes comes across as the ultimate attention seeker, but there was a telling scene in Houston after the last out had been recorded in the 2005 World Series. While his players jumped on one another in a celebratory pile, Guillen stayed in the dugout, where he and his three sons hugged. It was the players' time, he said, not his.

·3·

PROMOTE SERENITY IN THE WORKPLACE

Baseball is a macho sport, maybe the most macho sport. That might have something to do with the relative lack of physical contact between opponents, an idea that, on the face of it, seems contradictory. Football players can take out their frustrations by hitting each other. Same with hockey players. Basketball has become an increasingly physical game. But in baseball, there's rarely an occasion to elbow, punch, or tackle an opposing player. It's you against the other team, but mostly it's you against a spherical object wrapped tightly in cowhide. Hitters try to do violence to the ball, and most of the time they fail.

So baseball the most macho? Wouldn't the manliest sport be the one that involves the most ferocity? Not necessarily. The very lack of violence, or at least the lack of a regular outlet for violence, helps explain why irritated baseball players periodically look for things other than pitches to hit. There's a lot of compensating that goes on at the major-league level.

With the bases loaded in a game in early June 2011, Alex

Rios hit a ground ball back to Detroit Tigers pitcher Andrew Oliver. In something closer to homicidal rage than mere frustration, Rios responded by taking out his anger on a plastic bubblegum bucket in the White Sox dugout.

The incident called for subtlety from Guillen, who is to subtlety what Hugh Hefner is to abstinence. Ozzie is not a serial smasher of clubhouse and dugout items as a manager, though he did have a fairly lengthy rap sheet as a player. By his own count, in various fits of spleen during his playing career, he broke seven TVs, two Ping-Pong tables, a chair, a table, and some plumbing pipes.

This was the man who sat down with Rios to tell him he needed to be calmer in the future. It was the second time the manager had met with the center fielder during the season. The first was in late April, when Rios was stuck in a 2-for-26 slump, and Guillen wanted him to stop putting pressure on himself. Relax, he had told Rios. You have gobs of talent. You will prevail.

This meeting was for crimes against that bubblegum bucket, a fact that indicated the April meeting had not been very effective. If Rios had been hitting well, he wouldn't have had cause to smash a perfectly good plastic container. A 1-for-4 game that day had actually raised his batting average to .202.

Guillen hates bad body language. Usually that has to do with players who are sulking. In this case, he thought Rios was speaking a dialect of He's Completely Lost His Mind–ese, if not He's Going to Hurt Himself–ish. There's nothing to stop a ballplayer from getting mad. For many, a show of anger is the only way to show they care.

Ozzie could relate. He just couldn't tolerate it as a manager.

"I think he's too good to do that," Guillen said. "But I

understand. I was a player before. Sooner or later, you're going to go through it. Hopefully, that's the only day he shows me that. Everybody went through it. He's very frustrated that he can't help us. He's very upset because he can't do what he can to help us."

For all the focus fans and media put on a manager, he doesn't have much impact during a game. He doesn't decide if a player has a good day or a bad day. He doesn't decide where the ball goes off the bat. He has no say in a pitcher's ability to throw strikes. But Guillen believes he's responsible for a player's body language. He views bad body language or unruly emotions as something like a contagious disease. Teammates see a player with his head down, and suddenly their own heads get a little heavier. Teammates see a player losing control, and maybe their nerves tighten up that much more.

But if Guillen had to choose between a sulker and a player with anger issues, he'd hand a bat to the excitable one and tell him to have his way with the Gatorade container in the dugout. Players like White Sox rookie third baseman Brent Morel, who is as reserved as a banker's wardrobe, are a mystery to Guillen, who had been the opposite as a big-league ballplayer. But as long as you can play, he doesn't care if you have the personality of a store mannequin.

Rios promised Guillen he wouldn't act out anymore.

Like a lot of what Guillen says and does, there are gray areas. Huge, yawning gray areas. Gray areas that could accommodate a few baseball diamonds. Or, perhaps the better way to put it is: Do what Ozzie says, not what he did inside the visiting manager's office in Toronto.

The week before Rios's outburst, Guillen had taken out his frustration on a coffeemaker that, a few minutes earlier, had been minding its own business. He threw it against the wall. A chair got the same rough treatment. A combination of the White Sox' offensive inadequacies and a few players' impassive response to the fourteen-inning loss to the Blue Jays had sent him over the edge.

"First and third, no runs," he said later. "First and third, no runs. Second and third, no runs. I was pissed. The other thing I was pissed about, I walked into the room and a couple guys were acting like nothing happened."

That new ballpark in Miami—does it have sufficient property insurance?

The commotion in the manager's office in Toronto served as a loud message: this wasn't just another loss. There had been enough frustration in the first two months to fill an entire season. If the players didn't feel the way he did, maybe they were on the wrong team. This was Ozzie's way of letting them know that the ante was being raised, that baseball was as much about heart and desire as it was about talent. Tomorrow was indeed another day, but today wasn't over yet. Today sucked.

He had tried to protect his players from criticism, but he wanted their zeal, their commitment, their suffering in return. He knew they cared. But sometimes a manager wonders whether his players care as much as he does. Do they live and die with the game? Do the losses eat away at them? For Guillen, his professional life is good only when his team wins. A player can walk away from a loss and feel good about a 3-for-3 day at the plate. There is nothing like that for Guillen. It is black and white. Victory, good. Loss, bad. It's not the healthiest way to live, but it's the life he has chosen for himself.

Joey Cora had the misfortune of walking into the office when Guillen was erupting. He got hit in the leg by some unidentified flying object. He was surprised but unhurt.

That, of course, is one of the dangers of violent outbursts. Sometimes, the bubblegum container or the chair hits back. In September 2008, Guillen had watched the tightly wound Carlos Quentin slap his hand against his bat in anger after fouling off a fat, juicy pitch. It left him with a broken wrist and ended what might have been an MVP season. Quentin was leading the American League in home runs at the time.

"When you get hurt that way, you hurt the ball club," Guillen said. "You hurt yourself plus you're hurting twenty-five guys. And you're hurting the owner who has to pay you when you're hurt. . . . You regret it after you wake up and say, 'Wow, I shouldn't be doing that.' It's something we pray [they don't do]. We talk to people about it.

"There have been a lot of guys hurt because of, I don't want to say stupidity, but the passion and the tension of the game makes those guys do it. They know it's stupid, but in the meanwhile, when you're in that situation, that's the first thing that comes into your mind, and you do it. You wish you hadn't done it, but you can't control it."

He would know. In 1989, during the White Sox' first game at the team's new spring-training site in Sarasota, Florida, Guillen used a bat to beat up a bathroom after first baseman Frank Thomas had failed to catch one of Guillen's throws from short. It can't be overstated that this was a spring-training game, which, in the grand scheme of things, is like a reality TV show—there, but not filled with much meaning.

In 1997, he dropped an infield fly against the Tigers. When

the inning was over, he went into the clubhouse and took out his rage on a TV set. Most of that rage stemmed from the Sox' announcement earlier that day that they had traded Harold Baines, his closest friend on the team, to Baltimore.

Another time, a recliner in the clubhouse was the victim. Sadly, it was too late for a restraining order.

"That took me like seven fucking innings to break," Guillen said. "I went out on the field, come back, continue to hit it. I've got two more at-bats, and I continued to hit it.

"Every time we finished an inning, [teammate] Robin Ventura's right behind me. He was like, 'Holy shit.' He said, 'Are you done?' I said, 'Yeah.' He said, 'You've got a better swing inside than you do outside.' "

Besides coal mining, there aren't many professions that tolerate explosions. But baseball has a long history of fights, brawls, and general destruction. For a manager, it means having to be aware of a very fine line. You want your team to play with passion. You want your players to work along the far edges of emotions, where the difference between good and great sometimes lies. You don't want them to get hurt.

Baseball is a frustrating game with very few outlets for heightened enthusiasm. When an outlet does present itself, players sometimes can't help themselves. Again, Ozzie knows.

One time, the Sox' official scorer ruled that a ground ball Guillen barely touched was an error. When the inning was over, Guillen ran into the clubhouse and smashed a TV, causing a fire. When his teammates walked in, they found a white powder from the expired television covering their belongings.

Sometimes there's not a method to Guillen's madness. Sometimes there's just madness.

. . .

How does an Ozzie Guillen happen? A brash, emotional, motor-mouthed, impulsive, consequences-be-damned manager—how does that sort of person come about? Well, it's like what basketball coaches say about height: you can't teach it. People who grow to be seven-footers had no say in whether they were going to be seven feet tall. Ozzie could no more have become an introvert than Shaquille O'Neal could have become a point guard.

When Guillen arrived in the United States for rookie ball as a skinny seventeen-year-old in 1981, he was already a fully formed chatterer, 140 pounds of mouth. But he knew his baseball, or at least thought he did, and that informed most of what he said and did on the baseball field, even if it didn't always sit well with teammates and managers. He had already played against professionals in Venezuela. What was a collection of green ballplayers compared with that?

Jim Zerilla was the manager of the new Bradenton Padres of the Gulf Coast League. The year before, he had left the head coaching job at the University of Louisville to manage the San Diego Padres' affiliate in Walla Walla, Washington. This time, the parent club had dumped a bunch of signees on Zerilla and the big club's roving infield instructor Manny Crespo, along with a bunch of bats and balls.

Crespo was a former big-time Red Sox prospect whose career had been derailed by a knee injury. Neither he nor Zerilla knew a thing about the players the Padres had sent them.

"So I said to Manny, 'Okay, look, here's what we're going to do. We'll put all the infielders at short. You go out there with them, watch how they operate, how they move, whatever. I'll hit the ground balls, and you decide who should play where,' " Zerilla said.

"I'm hitting the ground balls, and all of a sudden Manny puts his hands up, 'Hold it!' And he calls Ozzie off to the side and talks to him for a few minutes. Then Manny tells me to start hitting again.

"We get done, and I said, 'Manny, what was going on?' He said, 'I had to tell Ozzie to cool it because he was telling all the other guys, 'Get off of shortstop. I'm the shortstop here. You guys don't belong.' That was Ozzie.

"Manny called him over and said, 'Look, that's not the way we do things. You've got to chill.' "

Ozzie chill? That's a good one.

The team was primarily made up of Americans, though there were about ten Latin players in the sixteen- to nineteen-year-old range on the roster. Some of the Latinos spoke a limited amount of English; others, including Ozzie, didn't. But he still had things to say.

"I grew up in baseball," Guillen said. "I knew what I had around me, and I knew I had more talent playing shortstop than anybody else. At that time, I knew for a fact I knew baseball more than they did. I saw how they moved.

"I had played with men before I came to the rookie league. I played in Venezuela for one year with Triple-A and big-league players before I came to the U.S. That's why I knew exactly what I had, who was next to me, and why guys were doing what. Not because I was better, just because I had more experience. I grew up in the game watching winter ball. I hung around with big-league players. I was a little above them, not in playing time, but in knowing the game better."

He knew where to position himself for different hitters.

He knew the most economical way to start a double play. He found himself explaining these things to other players. Maybe this was the flowering of a managerial career, but that's not how Guillen saw it. He saw it as a pain in the ass. More than that, he saw it as *pain*. Whenever someone made a mistake, Zerilla had the entire team run as punishment.

"That's why I hated those guys," Guillen said.

Part of the problem was cultural. He didn't fully understand how the system worked in the United States. He had been around big-league ballplayers, had heard about life in the majors, and had expectations of, well, more. And running? How was that supposed to get him to where he wanted to go?

He clashed at times with Zerilla.

"I said, 'This isn't baseball,'" Guillen said. "The problem we had, I didn't know he was coaching rookie league. I didn't know he was teaching kids. I thought it was a game we needed to win. Every time we got punished, I didn't like it. I told him, 'I've never seen that in baseball.' Running the bases until you die because we played bad? We didn't do that in Venezuela.

"A couple years later, I understood why he was making that point: we've got to learn baseball. But at the time, I couldn't understand why he was doing it. Why do we have a pitcher coaching first base? Why did we have forty players and the team is supposed to be twenty-five?

"I was asking all sorts of questions, and I didn't get the answers. Why did this guy play one day and I had to wait until the next day? I wanted to be the shortstop every day. It was hard for me to understand at the beginning of my career."

Nobody could hit well on the team. Besides being the manager, Zerilla was the team's third-base coach, too. He called the third-base coach's box the loneliest place in Bradenton, because none of his players ever got that far.

The Padres were losing to the Pirates' affiliate one day when Guillen hit a hard ground ball toward third base. The third baseman took two steps to his left and the ball hit off his glove and skittered into the outfield. When he got back to first base, Guillen yelled to a Padres pitcher who was keeping the score book in the dugout.

"Did you give me a hit or an error?"

"Error," the pitcher said.

That, of course, is not how Guillen saw it.

"Ozzie starts gibbering," Zerilla said. "Then he looks at me. I'm coaching third. I've got my arms crossed. He realizes, 'Uh-oh.' So he doesn't say anything else. After the game, I told everybody to get on the bus. I told Ozzie, 'Stay right here.'

"I jump into his crap pretty good, that you don't do that kind of stuff, that we're not here for you. The typical managerial speech. He gets tears in his eyes. I said, 'You know what? Go on the bus.' "

It looked as if Guillen's mouth had sunk his chances with the Padres. Zerilla went to Crespo with his frustrations.

"He said, 'I can't play this guy. He's only worried about himself,' " Crespo said. "I said, 'Z, he's not worried about himself, he's worried about winning. But when you're hitting .180, you need a hit.' He said, 'Well, I can't have that kind of guy.' I said, 'He's going to have to play.' "

Zerilla called Jack McKeon, then San Diego's vice president of baseball operations, and said he couldn't work with the kid.

Crespo called McKeon, too.

"If Ozzie goes, I gotta go," he told McKeon.

"What do you mean?" McKeon said.

"That's the reason I'm here—to help all the infielders, especially the Latin kids in their first year."

"I can't lose you," McKeon said.

"You can't lose this guy either."

Crespo had seen something in Guillen that he hadn't seen in many players. The kid didn't do anything particularly well. Crespo graded his fielding, throwing, hitting, power, and running as below average, compared with major-league players. But he wasn't a fully formed player yet, and he had a huge heart. He had worn Crespo out with his insistence on fielding one hundred extra ground balls a day. Crespo was so taken with the hardworking Venezuelan that he eventually gave a beloved baseball glove to him.

Crespo drew a line in the infield dirt: if Ozzie goes, so do I.

McKeon decided that Zerilla needed support from the Padres front office and that Guillen needed to be punished. Guillen would finish the season in Bradenton, but he wouldn't be allowed to play in the Fall Instructional League. Crespo thought the Padres were only punishing themselves, that Ozzie would benefit from another two months under his tutelage, but he understood the need for sanctions.

Still, Ozzie had to make things right with Zerilla. The day after the scoring incident, Zerilla had taken a piece of tape with Guillen's uniform number, 5, written on it and put it on the bench next to where the manager sat every game.

"He came out to get a ball to warm up," Zerilla said. "I said, 'Put the ball back in the bag. Do you see this number 5? Sit down here and don't move until September 1, the end of the season. You've got nothing to do but sit down.' I didn't play him that day.

"So he goes to Manny Crespo and says, 'Go tell Zerilla I'm sorry.' Manny said, 'No, you go tell Zerilla you're sorry.'"

Guillen eventually did, though Zerilla refused to take the piece of tape off the bench, in case the kid had a relapse of bad behavior. Guillen responded by hitting about .340 the rest of the season.

After all these years, the scoring incident is still fresh in Guillen's mind. He was in a hurry to get to the big leagues. Patience didn't have a chance. The minor leagues were the sacrificial cars in the path of the monster truck known as Ozzie.

He wanted something that was as big as his personality. He wanted it all. But first he wanted something much, much simpler.

"I wanted to get a hit, that's what it was," he said. "They had to understand I came there to make money and get out of the rookie league the best and quickest I could. They had to understand my point also. It wasn't because I wanted to disagree with the [scorer]. I just wanted to know what was in the scorecard. I thought it was a base hit. You know why? Because I know more than you in baseball. That was my point. My point was, I thought that was a pretty tough place to put an error. They didn't understand that point. To this day, I think it was a hit."

It doesn't take much to see the Ozzie of today in the seventeen-year-old Ozzie of 1981. Actually, it's not a matter of seeing. It's a matter of listening.

"Put youth with that personality and you can imagine," Zerilla said. "Just harmless stuff, but continuous chatter. He was always into something—the little kid you've got to always watch. There were times when some of his teammates would have liked to just grab him and said, 'Shut the hell up!' But he wasn't being malicious. It was his personality. It was him. It was Ozzie. He came that way, and he stayed that way. He came at seventeen to start his baseball career, and it hasn't changed."

The cartoonish image Guillen offers up of himself as a weak hitter tends to mask the truth of him as a talented, hardworking player. He'd arrive early at the team facility to get in extra work, Zerilla said. Guillen is quick to make fun of his hitting in the major leagues, but it wasn't as if he were a liability. He hit .264 during his career, was the 1985 American League Rookie of the Year, and was a three-time All-Star.

But the scrawny, blustery kid as a manager someday? Back then, you would have needed a high-powered telescope to see it.

"He was so skilled you knew that with any physical development he had the opportunity to be a great player," Zerilla said. "How do you look in the crystal ball and say a guy's going to be a manager? But even with the ease the game came to him, he would work. You hit him two hundred ground balls, he'll take a hundred more. You always said, 'Gee, this kid has a chance to do whatever he wants.'

"It was, would his personality get in the way of that? But the skill and determination to do whatever in baseball, that was always there. He did things naturally that nobody is going to teach. He was just one of those gifted guys. He could make every play. There would be moments where you said, 'Jesus, I don't believe I just saw that.' He could do anything fielding. The first summer I had him, he could hit. He was smart enough to understand that he wasn't going to hit it far, he just needed to put it in play."

Guillen laughs when he thinks of those days.

"You know what's so bad?" he said. "One day, I talked to Manny Crespo. I said, 'Tell Zerilla if I coach or manage one day in my life, I hope one of his fucking kids or grandkids or anybody with the last name Zerilla goes through my system to see fucking how bad they're going to have to run.' "

Take this intelligent, combustible human being and mix him with authority figures. You're going to get—what's the word?—*friction*.

"I like all umpires," Guillen insists.

Of course he's going to say that, right? He has to work with these people.

"Wrong," he says. "I'm not a hypocrite. I like maybe 98 percent of the umpires. I do. As long as you're fair."

When Guillen steps onto the field to argue a call, he's ready to accept two of three possibilities: the umpire will admit he was wrong or the umpire will talk back. Either is fine. Nothing wrong with mistakes, and nothing wrong with disagreements.

The third possibility, that the umpire will allow no discussion, is enough to ignite Ozzie's rocket boosters. That possibility presented itself in late April 2011, when the White Sox were in New York for a three-game series against the Yankees. Yankee Stadium is not the place to be when you're trying to right a listing ship, but the Sox had won the first two games of the series against the Bronx Bombers, and there was a sliver or two of sunlight attempting to cut through the gloom caused by the ten losses the team had suffered in the eleven games before that.

The mess started with a failure to communicate, which is

hard to believe with the übercommunicative Guillen. When Paul Konerko struck out looking to end the top of the first inning, Guillen yelled at home plate umpire Todd Tichenor not to cave in to Yankees manager Joe Girardi, who had complained about the previous pitch, which Tichenor had called a ball.

"The one thing coming out of my mouth was, 'Don't let those guys intimidate you,'" Guillen said. "But he couldn't hear me because I was too far away. When I go out there to tell him what I said, he said, 'Do not come onto the field.' That's when everything started. That's when I got pissed."

It was also about the time Tichenor threw him out of the game.

Although umpires have a low tolerance for it, a manager can come out of the dugout to discuss what he might consider to be an inconsistent strike zone. But Guillen didn't want to talk about Tichenor's eyesight. He wanted to talk about what he perceived to be Tichenor's jellylike spine. Surely you can see the distinction.

One of the unwritten rules in baseball is that an umpire can't order a manager to stay in the dugout. He can say, "If I have to throw you out of the game, I will," or something to that effect. Tichenor tossed Guillen when he stepped out of the dugout, which is why Ozzie looked as if he were trying to run from a swarm of bees as he sprinted toward the umpire.

He became truly enraged when Tichenor, a minor-league call-up, walked away from him in mid-rant. Depriving Guillen of what he does best? You call this a democracy?

Later, a bit removed from the incident, he still saw the immediate ejection as a lack of respect.

"Don't tell me not to come onto the field like you're going

to intimidate me," he said. "I'm supposed to say, 'Okay, I'm sorry, I won't go onto the field'?

"First of all, you're not my father. I know the rules. When you say, 'Don't come on the field,' you're challenging me. You challenge me in the wrong way. He thought I was arguing about strikes and balls. I went out to tell him, 'Don't let those guys intimidate you.'

"He didn't understand what I was saying. Besides, I was sick. I had a cold. I couldn't even fucking talk. I said, 'How the hell did you hear what I said? You can't even hear me now.' "

Tichenor couldn't hear him? In Guillen's book, there are fewer things more tragic. But this being a technologically advanced world, there was a solution. Before the first inning was over, Guillen had tweeted his indignation from his place of banishment.

"This one going to cost me a lot money this is patetic."

And a bit later: "Today a tough guy show up a yankee stadium," referring to Tichenor.

Giving Guillen a Twitter account is like handing a bomber a remote detonator.

The next day, Major League Baseball suspended Guillen for two games and fined him $20,000 for tweeting while the game was still in progress and for criticizing an umpire. It was the first time in league history a manager had been fined for a tweet. And to think, two weeks before, Guillen had said he didn't use his Twitter account for anything having to do with his team. It was like a lot of what Ozzie says: subject to change.

He learned of the sanctions after the White Sox had returned home from New York. He stood in a tunnel leading to the Sox clubhouse, still trying to make sense of what had happened.

"The reason I tweeted was I thought, 'This motherfucker thinks he's going to get away with that,'" he said. "The tweet wasn't bad. The timing of the tweet was bad."

So here was another Ozzie explosion on full public display. The smoke drifted over the country. People gawked. Bystanders pointed at the excitable manager running headlong into another controversy.

His wife, Ibis, didn't know about the fine yet, but he knew how she'd react.

"She will be pissed," he said.

But surely $20,000 is walking-around money for someone of Guillen's means?

"Yeah, my ass," he said.

By the time he met the media an hour later, he had turned into Contrite Ozzie.

"I learned a lesson," he said.

The moral of the story? If at all possible, remain calm. That's the message Guillen charges himself with spreading as a manager. Remain calm, unless you can't. Then go to Twitter.

Guillen will do a lot of things to shake up his team, but he doesn't believe a manager's ejection has much value, even when the losses are piling up like driftwood in a dam.

"A lot of people think so, but when you get kicked out of the game, it doesn't help," he said. "You go out there because you have to protect your player, but in the meanwhile you leave the players by themselves. I don't think that's good for anyone. Sometimes you have to, because of your players. But it's never a benefit. That's why they kick you out. It's a punishment."

When a manager is banished to the clubhouse, it means a coach takes over the team. It can be like a substitute filling in for an absent teacher.

"For some reason, people lose intensity when the manager's gone," Guillen said. "Ninety-nine percent of the people lose intensity. It's a different feeling."

Asked whether he would ever consider pulling a base out of its moorings during an argument with an umpire, the way Billy Martin and Lou Piniella might have done it, Guillen was adamant.

"Hell, fuck no," he said. "I'm not going to waste my time. I don't want to be embarrassed. In my arguments with the umpires, I never kicked dirt."

Dirt, maybe not. A catcher's mask, yes. Seven weeks later, Guillen came storming out of the dugout in the sixth inning of a game against the Cubs. Alexei Ramirez had chopped a ball into the dirt and watched it spin back behind the plate. Cubs catcher Geovany Soto picked up the ball and tagged Ramirez. Home plate umpire James Hoye ruled that Soto had picked it up before it rolled behind the plate, meaning it was a fair ball and therefore that Ramirez was out. Here came Guillen. He had had what he thought was a perfect vantage point of the play from where he was standing in the Sox dugout.

He angrily pointed at a spot behind the plate where Soto's mitt seemed to have disturbed the dirt as he picked up the ball. Hoye kicked Guillen out of the game. Guillen responded by kicking Soto's mask about ten feet. It was Piniella-worthy. Or Pele-worthy.

In hindsight, *some* event was inevitable that night. Game 1 of the always emotional Cubs-Sox series. A big crowd on hand. Many more media members in attendance than for a typical game at the Cell. It was too enticing for someone given to big statements and big gestures. Of course that mask lying on the ground was going to get kicked. It was practically asking for it. Soto couldn't help himself when he saw it go flying. He laughed.

Afterward, with Guillen exiled in the Sox clubhouse, there were no tweets, the way there had been in New York. See? Ozzie is capable of learning lessons.

"He was right, and I was wrong," Guillen told reporters after the game, rolling his eyes. "Because if I say what I want to say, it's another twenty thousand dollars. I'm tired of paying people money for no reason."

There was also another lesson.

"If I kicked a mask twenty years ago, I might have broken my toe," he said. "They make the mask so light and so good now that I didn't feel anything."

And what about Guillen's theory that a manager's ejection doesn't do much to rally his players? The Cubs beat the Sox 6–3 that night. And the Yankees had beaten the Sox the day Ozzie got kicked out and fired off his critical tweets.

He argues with umpires to prove a point, but he never wins. Never. No manager does. Baseball uses instant replay only in very specific situations limited to home runs. The umpire is still king.

Guillen is generally respectful of umpires. He understands the difficulty of making split-second decisions, especially in an era in which people at home can see replays instantly. He tries to keep umps on their toes, to make them remember that he and his team are to be respected, too. If he gets any hint that the umpire believes he, the man in the gray pants, is the reason thousands of baseball fans have streamed through the turnstiles, God help him.

Ozzie will do what he did in 2010 to Joe West, the pig-nosed, country music–singing umpire who isn't averse to yanking the spotlight his way. During a game in Cleveland, West tossed Guillen after the manager had gone out to argue a balk call against Mark Buehrle. Guillen thought West was simply looking for attention, and he got it by being what Guillen viewed as dismissive and disrespectful.

In front of 18,109 fans, Ozzie dropped the lineup card at West's feet.

"I said, 'You want people to focus on you? Here, you be the manager and then everybody come to see you,'" Guillen said. "I said, 'Here, take it. You want to be manager, or you want to be a baseball player? Here, motherfucker.' I dropped it right in front of him, and he started laughing."

Guillen actually likes West for the way he controls a game, for the way he carries himself like a cop in a one-cop town. He makes a call and considers it law. Maybe Ozzie likes him because he sees a little bit of himself in West, who enjoys a crowd.

One time, Guillen held up his right arm to signal he was making a pitching change even though, at the same time, he told West he was bringing in a left-hander. Technically, the gesture meant he wanted a right-hander from the bullpen, but most umpires let a manager's mental confusion slide. Not West, who made Guillen bring in a righty.

"Sometimes he wants to show you he knows more about baseball," Guillen said. "I said, 'You're just big-leaguing me.' And he was. And he was wrong. But I had to stick with the right-hander because Joe said it was the rules. That's not the rules because the next day I see another manager do the same shit. But I went by whatever he wanted. You talk about controlling the game. He controls the game very well."

If Guillen believes an umpire is having an unusually bad day or an unusually bad career, he'll trot out the nuclear weapon: complete disdain. He'll run onto the field with the feigned intention of arguing a call, get halfway there, stop, throw his hands up to show that he has decided he has better things to do than argue with an obviously inept umpire, and walk back to the dugout.

"I did it twice in 2010," he said. "I did it in Detroit, and I did it in Chicago. That shit pisses them off. In Detroit, I run to the middle of the field, and I go, 'Ah, fuck it, I'm not going to waste my time.' On the way back, the third-base umpire says, 'Fucking asshole! You're a piece of shit, Ozzie!' I say, 'Yeah, how about him?' "

He did it again in 2011 during a game against the Twins at the Cell. He took six or seven steps, thought better of it, did his "I'm done with you" gesture, and returned to the dugout.

Is it worth it? Does it pay off? Probably not, but sometimes a manager has to react. There's a certain satisfaction in making a point, even if it might hurt you in the checkbook or down the road with the same umpire. It's a sport with long pauses built in. There's more inaction than action. It's why players and managers are so quick to react when there's even a hint of conflict.

And the best stories seem to come from conflict. Or near-miss conflicts.

When Guillen was playing for the White Sox in the late 1980s, manager Jim Fregosi came out of the dugout to argue a call by first-base umpire Durwood Merrill at old Comiskey Park in Chicago. When Merrill saw Fregosi, he turned and trotted to right field to let the manager know he didn't have time for any nonsense. And Fregosi wasn't going to chase him.

Guillen waited for Fregosi in the dugout.

"That piece of shit!" Fregosi screamed. "I'll get him tomorrow! Fuck him! He's not going to embarrass me like that!"

"Uh, Jim?"

"What!"

Guillen waited a beat.

"Tomorrow we play in Boston."

·4·

GET RID OF THE CLUTTER IN THEIR HEADS

The Marlins have a psychologist on their payroll. His job is to counsel players who have asked for help.

It's a good thing, right? Professional athletes experience enormous stress, and having an outlet can offer relief. Who among us could be against positive thoughts? Who could be against the work of psychologists when gaining a mental edge has become so popular in sports?

Funny you should ask.

"When I was playing the game, nothing was mental," Guillen said. "All of a sudden, everything's mental—'Attention deficit, I got problems. I need to talk to a psychologist.' Bullshit. That's a bunch of shit. That's an excuse, like it's mental. You suck.

"Mental? Well, why isn't it mental when you go 4-for-4? You got the same brains. I don't believe players have mental problems. If you have a physical problem, there are doctors, and they tell you you can't play. You have mental problems, you can play baseball. To me, that's an excuse."

The study of psychology, which has worked many a man through his hatred of his father, is periodically in Ozzie's crosshairs, at least as it relates to sports. Usually, by the time he's done, sports psychology is experiencing profound feelings of inadequacy. Never mind that the White Sox' psychologist had earnestly plied his craft and dealt with some very fragile psyches throughout the 2011 season. Adam Dunn had gone to see him. Had, in fact, played golf with him. If God had intended for baseball players to use sports psychologists, He would have told Abner Doubleday about them, and as far as Guillen could tell, He hadn't.

Ozzie regularly brings players into his office to offer counsel and to listen to their problems. Dunn, Alex Rios, and Brent Morel had listened to his encouragement during the 2011 season. So had Gordon Beckham and Alexei Ramirez. A mental-health therapist might suggest that Ozzie's aversion to team psychologists is easy to explain. He thinks he's the only psychologist his players need. Anything to do with his players at the ballpark is his bailiwick, nobody else's.

For all the pats on the back he gives and for all the words of encouragement he offers, Dr. Oz's bottom-line message is stark: it's up to you. You have to rescue yourself from your problems. In the end, you are the only one who can make your life better.

Guillen is very much into self-determination, especially at the plate. When he talks about hitters being the loneliest people on the planet when they're facing pitchers, he is correct. Those might not be the most comforting words in the world, but they're accurate. When you're waiting for a pitcher to throw the baseball, there's no one to phone for help, no lifeline to grab. And when the ball is zooming toward you with your embarrassment as its only goal in life, a psychologist can't swing the bat for you.

"It's all about you," Guillen said. "You can call Mom, you can call Dad, your college coach, your high school coach, but when you go to the plate, you're alone. You're by yourself. It doesn't help you when you talk to people. You want people to make you feel better, but I don't think that helps at all.

"You call your mom and you say, 'Mommy, I'm struggling.' What the fuck is she going to say? 'Go get it'? Or, 'You'll be okay'? I don't believe in that. I believe in players going out there and being mentally strong to compete. I don't think calling anybody helps."

Sports psychology has become a huge business. Practitioners call themselves by various names: sports psychologist, athletic mental conditioning coach, performance enhancement expert, and so on. Athletes in all sports and at all levels use them. When Guillen half-kiddingly says that managers and coaches are the ones in need of counseling, he might be right. They have the weakest grip on the outcome of a game, and they might experience the deepest feelings of helplessness.

He brought this up in May 2011, when Dunn and Rios were into their second month of struggles. Who, Guillen wanted to know, was going to help hitting coach Greg Walker's mental state? Every time Dunn struck out, fans called for Walker's firing, if not his outright execution.

"What can we do?" Guillen said. "Every time they go to the plate or to the mound, you think, 'Wow, I hope they do good because I don't want to get fired.' Hey, man, [the coaches] need the mental guys. We need a little vacation to go somewhere else to recover.

"Those guys get to go out and fight every day. They get to

fight. That's the thing. The players are the pilots. We are sitting in the back of the airplane. If we're going to crash, the plane's going to crash because it's their fault, but I'm going to crash, too. I'm going to be the first to die, but I'm not driving the plane."

At the time, a sportswriter suggested to Guillen that perhaps he might want to pay a visit to the team psychologist. After all, the Sox had lost sixteen of their previous twenty games. If that wasn't a situation crying out for intensive therapy, what was?

The thought of an unsuspecting mental-health professional working on Ozzie's bigger-than-life personality is an irresistible one. It's like wondering how a watermelon dropped from a tenth-story window would fare against a sidewalk.

"That guy, if he took me on, he will retire," Guillen said, smiling. "He will quit. I guarantee you, he will quit. To me, mental? Those [players] are in the big leagues for a reason. I don't get it. Before, I never heard that. This is my twenty-fifth year in the big leagues. The mental problems started like five years ago. Before, we used to solve a mental problem with vodka and a lot of Budweiser."

If you're looking to establish your business's core values, you could do a lot worse than "vodka and a lot of Budweiser."

"People say, 'Be positive,'" Guillen said. "When you go to the plate, you don't even know what the [psychologist's] name is. Nothing against the guy. I respect him because this man went to school and he wants to help us. But I think right now, everything is an excuse."

Early in the 2011 season, Juan Pierre had dropped two balls in the outfield, costing the Sox two games. Guillen did not call him into his office. He didn't talk with him about the errors.

He talked with him about anything but those errors. There was psychology in that.

"If I say something to Juan, he's going to think I'm panicking or I don't have any confidence in him," he said privately at the time.

If it had been Morel, the quiet rookie, or Ramirez, the talented, still-developing shortstop, Guillen would have made a beeline for them. He would have told them the errors didn't matter, that they were in the past, that today was another day. But there was a fragility to those players that was nonexistent in Pierre.

Pierre had absorbed a lot of fan abuse over the years, especially while with both Chicago teams and with the Los Angeles Dodgers. He didn't look like a ballplayer. It was as if someone had taken a little kid's head and attached it to a man's body, and the end product didn't resemble people's image of a big-league outfielder. At times, neither did his play. But Guillen admired the nobility with which Pierre carried himself, even as the vitriol flew from the stands.

When Pierre went to Matt Thornton to apologize for the two errors that had led to two blown saves for the Sox reliever, Guillen said it wasn't necessary, but the gesture made him appreciate the man even more. That's the kind of attitude that helps teams, he believed. It's the reason Guillen was dead set against bringing up Dayan Viciedo from Triple-A to replace Pierre, even when Pierre's batting average was threatening to fall below .200.

And Pierre would reward Ozzie's faith. By mid-August he was hitting .285.

Guillen rarely says anything to players who make mistakes on the field, as long as the mistakes aren't rooted in a lack of effort. If he were to yell at an infielder who makes an error, he believes, that player would likely be as tight as a piano wire the next time a ground ball came his way. When a player is afraid to make mistakes, you can count on him making more in short order.

And yet coaches forever have been screaming at players who slip up. "Spare the rod and spoil the child" is still very much alive in sports. It wears a toe tag in Guillen's clubhouse.

"I've always had this philosophy that you are out there to make mistakes," he said. "The only people who don't make mistakes are the people not playing. There's not much you can do about it, whether you're a veteran or a kid. I think it's harder for the kid to handle because the kid is going to feel more guilty about it. His feelings are going to hurt more than the veteran. The veteran has been there before. A veteran can handle himself better with the media and the fans. You let them keep playing, and you believe and you trust them."

Part of Guillen's refusal to bench Adam Dunn was financial. A few months into the season, he wasn't going to bench a designated hitter whose salary was $12 million. But he truly believed that if he continued to show faith in Dunn and the other struggling players, they would produce. And what was a sports psychologist's approval compared with a manager's encouragement? Or a manager's stress-busting humor?

In June, after giving Dunn a two-game break from his struggles, Guillen had put him back in the lineup but not without some faux pleading.

"I just told him, 'Can you please have a good day? Then I don't have to answer all the questions about you. Please have a good day so Greg Walker doesn't have to drink a bottle of wine under your name to forget about your bad night.'"

Dunn rewarded Ozzie's faith with a two-run homer. And yet those kinds of giddy moments were few and far between. But Guillen did not feel sorry for Dunn, did not pity him. There's no room for that in Guillen's thinking. When a player signs a big contract, he signs up for everything that goes with it—the money, the huge expectations, the boos, the adulation, and the lack of privacy. Dunn was a big boy with a bull's-eye on his back. He would have to handle it. In the end, he would have to handle it on his own.

"That's why when you hit .250 and you play a hundred years in the big leagues, nobody cares about you," Guillen said. "When you hit .390, and you start making fifty, sixty million, you're a target. That's why my life in baseball was great. Nobody expected me to do anything. I never was booed in the big leagues. Why? Because they knew I was another guy in the field. I wasn't a superstar. I just played my game."

Some players can't handle the burden of expectations. It's not an easy thing to go from being a very good player on a so-so team to being a key component on a team chasing a pennant. Guillen is convinced there are big leaguers who freeze up at the mere thought of it.

"Some players don't like to compete," he said. "Some players get traded to a winning team, and they don't like that. I guarantee they don't. They might say, 'Yeah, I like it.' Bullshit. They like to play 162 games, play the game, but when you go to trade guys to put them in a good situation to win, some people can't handle that. You can win with your own team, but when you go someplace else and all of a sudden you're the man to help us, it's not an easy thing to handle. It's not."

Guillen wasn't talking about Alex Rios, but the center fielder almost fit the description. He had been a two-time All-Star in low-pressure Toronto but was better known for swearing at a heckling fan in 2009. The Sox got him off waivers later that season, and he hit .199 in forty-one games. He bounced back in 2010 with a .284 average, twenty-one home runs, and eighty-eight runs batted in. Then came the disaster of the 2011 season.

By design, there's something very laissez-faire about the way Guillen runs a ball club. He looks very hands-on as a manager because he appears to be everywhere at once, jabbering all the while. But he often holds the steering wheel with his knees. He keeps his players on a very loose rope. His job is to believe in them. Their job is to live up to that belief.

Rios hadn't. He hadn't played well, and, worse, he had the dreaded lack-of-hustle incident on his permanent record. It was why Guillen pulled him from a game at the end of June.

Football coaches are micromanagers. They deal in details. They deal in details of details, down to how every minute of a two-hour practice will be used. They wear headsets during games. Ozzie tries to wear a look of patience. He wants his players to hear a tiny voice in their heads—a tiny voice with a thick Venezuelan accent—telling them that at least one person who matters has their backs.

"A lot of people think a manager's job is writing the lineups and talking with the media and putting on the hit-and-run," Guillen said. "The manager's hardest job is to make sure the players know you're there for them."

When he walked away from Chicago and headed to Miami, it was one of the things he felt best about. He had stood by Dunn, even if it hadn't paid off.

Ozzie does believe in the power of positive thinking, and

he'll need it with a Marlins team that finished last in the National League East in 2011 with a 72–90 record. No matter how bad things get during a game, he refuses to cave in to negativity. Something good is right around the corner—he's sure of it—even if things look grim. He makes himself believe that. Others can't do it.

"It's why a lot of coaches drink, smoke, get ulcers," he said. "I don't got anything."

Well, that's not entirely true. In June, he got kidney stones, which have been described as bringing on the most pain a human can experience this side of childbirth. But you won't find stress or negativity listed as a cause for them.

The stones could have been Minnesota Twins–induced, however.

To say the Twins had the White Sox' number in recent years doesn't do justice to the carnage. In 2009 and 2010, Minnesota won twenty-five of thirty-six games against the Sox. In 2011, the Twins won seven of the first eight games between the two teams.

No one could fully explain the degree of domination. It's not as if the Twins had been a great team or even a more talented team than the Sox. But baseball people gush about how Minnesota plays the game "the right way." If the Twins ever go out of existence, that will be carved on their gravestone: they played the game the right way.

What it means is that players at all levels of the Twins' minor-league system are taught to play the game the same way. They learn to bunt the same way. The signals at Single-A ball are the same at the major-league level. Everything is uniform so that when a young player is brought up to the big leagues, his comfort level is higher and, the thinking goes, he will play better.

It still doesn't explain how the Twins had beaten the Sox so regularly and so relentlessly. If it were all about the continuity of their minor-league system, Minnesota would beat everybody all the time.

"If Minnesota doesn't play the White Sox, they're done," Guillen said. "They'd be selling everything. They're out of the pennant race, they're done. But they're playing us, so they're still in the pennant race."

In July, when the Twins were busy doing what they usually do to the Sox, winning three of four games, a TV reporter asked Guillen whether it was time to verbally challenge his players. Wouldn't it be helpful for Ozzie to stand in front of his team like a latter-day Vince Lombardi and ask out loud whether anyone in the clubhouse was sick of losing to Minnesota?

"No," he said. "I talk to my kids like that. I don't talk to baseball players like that. They're not my kids. I hope they are tired of losing to those guys. I hope they're embarrassed about losing to those guys. But what are you going to do? Get a pep rally and all of a sudden get your ass kicked again?

"This is not a football game, like you get pumped up for one day and hitting everything. This is day by day. It's not a football game where you go out there and play once a week and try to kill each other on Sundays. No, this is a mental, tough game. A lot of people don't think it is.

"You have to be very tough mentally to play this game 162 times—or to come here 162 times. That's the way it is. What am I going to tell them? They're not kids. They know what they're doing."

If a baseball manager gave rah-rah speeches intended to pump up his players for battle before each game, his team would be emotionally spent a quarter of the way through the season. Speeches meant to make players want to tear out of the clubhouse and onto the field don't help them hit a baseball. Speeches might make them want to knock the ball out of the catcher's mitt during a collision at home plate, but they won't help them hit a curveball. And they won't make them beat the Twins.

To make a career out of baseball, a player has to overcome the tedium of his existence. It takes a resolve made of Kevlar. Off days are rare in the major leagues. Every day is basically the same. Get to the ballpark three or four hours before the game. Answer questions from reporters in the clubhouse. Play cards. Lift weights. Run. Stretch. Take batting practice. Shag balls if you're not hitting. Take grounders if you're an infielder. Sit around some more. Stand and take off your cap for another rendition of the national anthem by someone who goes 0-for-4 on the high notes. Play the game. Answer more questions. Take a shower. Maybe taste the nightlife. Go home; go to sleep. Get up and do it again the next day.

Aside from rain or injury, nothing breaks that routine.

"Do you know how hard it is every day to get up and play baseball?" Guillen said. "It's hard. Every day, for all summer. It drags you down. Sometimes you don't want to get out of bed and do it. You have to deal with the same stuff and the same routine. That's 162 plus spring training. That's 192 times. Mentally, you've got to be tough."

The game of football doesn't bother Guillen. Football as it relates to baseball bothers Guillen. A lot. Baseball is a wonderfully intricate, inbred game that moves to its own rhythm.

It's a unique entity, and Guillen bristles at what he sees as attempts at crossbreeding. There's a reason many players kick around in the minor leagues for years before they get a chance at the bigs. They have to be programmed or deprogrammed, depending on the individual. They have to be transformed, indoctrinated.

When the White Sox draft an American player who has also starred in football, Guillen's sphincter gets a little tighter. Dual-sport athletes might not fully fathom the demands of playing baseball for a living, specifically the mental demands.

"I hate when people say, 'Wow, this is a good athlete,'" he said. "Well, he's not a goddamn baseball player. Good athlete does not mean good ballplayer. To play baseball, you have to be a good baseball player, not a good athlete. That's why you see a lot of baseball players who weigh three hundred pounds—fat, no muscles—because they're good baseball players, not because they're good athletes."

The idea that a football player can come in and, with enough time, become an accomplished baseball player galls Guillen to no end. Give him a player who has been weaned on baseball, who sleeps with his bat. That's his kind of player, even though he was a volleyball star growing up in Venezuela.

"I've never seen a good football player play good baseball," he said. "Never. Never. Maybe one that I remember: Brian Jordan. Bo Jackson sucked playing baseball. Deion Sanders sucked playing baseball. [The White Sox] put Bo Jackson in, and everybody [treated him like] Mr. Baseball and shit, but it was always, 'He *could have* been a good baseball player.' A football player can't play baseball. They tried before and that shit didn't happen. Name me somebody. Joe Borchard was a great quarterback in college, sucked playing baseball. Josh

Fields is a great quarterback, sucks in baseball. What football player came to play baseball and you say, 'Wow, look at this guy'?"

When Ozzie gets on a roll like this, it's hard to stop him. But Lou Gehrig played football at Columbia University. The general consensus seems to be that he turned out all right as a baseball player. Before Kirk Gibson hit one of the most memorable home runs in baseball history for the Dodgers, he was a football star at Michigan State University. Adam Dunn was a quarterback at the University of Texas before he decided to concentrate on baseball. And so on.

Guillen's bigger point probably can be applied to any sport. The more time you spend with one sport after high school, the better you'll be at it. And nothing prepares a baseball player for the mental rigors of the game than playing and practicing it over and over again.

And then following that up with extra batting practice.

"I gotta lot of respect for [football players]," Guillen said. "I can't play football. I don't think a lot of players can play football. In the meanwhile, this is a tough game. You guys think it is easy? Well, show up every day and do it. Take it from me. I was here every day playing. It's not easy."

In 2006, during one of his daily verbal wanderings, Guillen said he could par a hole in a PGA Tour event before Tiger Woods could get a base hit in a major-league baseball game. Woods said he would take him up on that bet, which, of course, could never be resolved. But underneath the laughs was dead seriousness by Ozzie. No sport is as difficult as baseball, both mentally and physically, unless you are talking about his first love, bullfighting, in which case you'd best genuflect. Ask Michael Jordan about baseball. He played in the White Sox' minor-league system after his first retirement from basketball and failed.

"One of the best athletes in the United States tried playing baseball and sucked," Guillen said. "Baseball is a different thing, man. Baseball is a very tough sport. Football, they beat the shit out of each other for three hours, and they got defense, offense, quarterback, kicker. Here, when you go to the plate, you go there by yourself. When you go to pitch, you're there by yourself. Nobody's helping you do it."

The TV reporter, the one who had asked Ozzie if it might be time for a Knute Rockne speech to wake up his players against the Twins, wondered out loud whether the Sox simply needed to be mentally tougher. Guillen's raised eyebrows seemed to suggest that critical mass had finally been reached and that everyone and his brother were now baseball experts.

Or maybe he had stumbled upon his own private sports psychologist.

"You know what? I'm going to hire you as a fucking coach to see if you can fucking help me," he said.

He didn't need to. The Twins uncharacteristically crashed and burned in 2011, losing ninety-nine games and ending up in last place in the division.

Players-only meetings are a kind of group therapy, only without an hourly rate. Players get to bitch about whatever it is that's bothering them, whether it be an outfielder who only seems to care about himself or a shortstop who is more concerned with talking with the media than with running hard to first base.

It can be cathartic, with players getting a better understanding of their teammates' feelings. It can also be painful, with players finding out exactly what their teammates think of them. The idea is to get all the bad feelings out on the table, bring about some positive change, and move on, ideally to more victories.

The day before the 2011 season began in Cleveland, Guillen called his own meeting, the theme of which was that he didn't want to have any more meetings the rest of the season. In his mind, meetings are for losers. Meetings always mean something's wrong. A manager doesn't call a team meeting to congratulate his players on their combined on-base percentage or to compliment them on their support of the wives' clothing drive. No, a team meeting means trouble has established a beachhead.

As much as Guillen did not want team gripe sessions, he knew there would be rough times in a long, grinding season. And thus meetings would be necessary to address problems and air grievances. There is an art to conducting a meeting, a management skill some say requires a glassblower's touch. Guillen's approach resembles a blacksmith's forearms.

"One thing I've learned. Don't ever have a meeting when you lose a fucking game," he says. "Nobody wants to hear your shit. Just wait for your time. When you win and everybody's happy, then you fucking have the meeting. You say, 'Listen motherfuckers, yeah we win today, but here are the problems: A, B, C, D.' "

To have a team meeting after a defeat is to ensure that the manager will not have the attention of the players. If Ozzie can't have the attention of his audience and if his message doesn't sink in, what's the point of living?

"We won a game, and I had a meeting after the fucking media left. I told Joey Cora, 'Nobody fucking leave the clubhouse,'" he says. "As soon as the media left, we fucking talked. I went out and talked to their wives and said, 'I'm sorry, I apologize. Does your husband need a ride? I'll take him home. But they've got to stay here for another hour.'

"We had a meeting. They agreed with me. Everybody went home happy. I went home happy. Let's fucking do this shit. But as soon as you lose a game and you're going to call out your motherfucking people? They say, 'I don't want to hear your shit, motherfucker. You think we're fucking happy about fucking losing the game?' No."

He broke his own team-meeting rule early in the 2010 season. The team huddled together as Ozzie talked, begged, pleaded, and cajoled. The Sox had started poorly that season, as well. They had just lost 12–0 to Tampa Bay, and if Guillen was sure of one thing, it was that he couldn't exist in a clubhouse that felt like after-school detention. He needed his clubhouse to be alive with music and chatter, with loud card games and practical jokes.

He addressed the team.

"I said, 'Listen, I don't want to do this, but I need to talk as a friend. I need to talk as a guy behind you,'" he said. "Because if I didn't do it, I might not sleep.

"I said, 'Hey, I see a lot of long faces, a lot of worries, a lot of bad at-bats. Just erase everything you did for the last twelve games, thirteen to fifteen games. Start over. I want to see a smile on your face. The clubhouse is very quiet, and I don't like that because we're going to spend a lot of time together and I want to be happy. I want to laugh through the tough times.'

"I told them, 'It's easy when you're good and everything's

going good for you. It's hard when you're down on the ground and you don't know how to get up. It's hard to play this game. Just make it as easy as you can and put a smile on your face. The only thing I ask is go out there and give me your best effort.' "

Whatever kind of meeting it was, it was called more for the manager's peace of mind than for the players' edification. It didn't seem to help much immediately, but the players did loosen up. And the clubhouse felt like happy hour later in the season when the Sox won twenty-six of thirty-one games.

All team meetings are different. That one was called to calm the players' psyches and make Ozzie feel better. The one Guillen called before a game near the end of the 2009 season, a get-together that lasted twenty-five minutes, had one theme.

"He told everybody we suck," Mark Buehrle said.

The Sox responded by losing 11–0 to the Royals.

If Guillen has learned one thing, it's that sometimes trying harder makes things worse. If a hitter strangles the bat handle before the pitch, he'll forget to breathe, or some other necessity. If you try harder in hockey or soccer, it often pays off. Not in baseball. It's often the reverse: you slide backward. Most of Guillen's team meetings are not called to tell his players they suck.

"Of all the times he's ever talked to us as a group, 99 percent of the time it's been about tapering it back and relaxing and taking it easy, as opposed to let's go, we need a kick in the ass," Konerko said. "There's only been one or two of those in his time here. It's always been the opposite, telling everybody, 'Back off here for a second. Let's have some fun. Let's go out tonight.'

"People on the outside might look at him and think it would

be the opposite. Even guys we play against think he's hard to play for, like he's tough, that if you don't do the job, he's yelling at you. It's not like that at all. The only time I've ever seen him get a rise is when a guy doesn't run a ball out."

The team meeting to open the season is a different animal entirely. Optimism is everywhere. It resides in every city that has a major-league franchise. But in the case of the 2011 White Sox, the optimism seemed to be warranted. They had the potential to be a World Series team, like the one Guillen had led in 2005. If everyone could stay healthy, a rotation of Mark Buehrle, John Danks, Gavin Floyd, Edwin Jackson, and Jake Peavy looked as if it would be able to keep the Sox in most games.

Guillen stood in front of the players with his reading glasses on—"little old lady glasses," A. J. Pierzynski called them—so that he could read his notes. Some of his thoughts were meant for newcomers like Dunn, who was expected to bring those forty home runs and one hundred runs batted in to the lineup. Guillen told them about Chicago, about the media, about expectations. He told them to develop thick skin quickly, even though there are times you can poke a toothpick through his.

He stood in front of his team and asked them—begged them—to let him be the center of attention, for their own good, of course.

"Every time he has a meeting, you laugh a lot because he says things that you really don't expect to hear in a meeting," Omar Vizquel said.

Such as?

"Can't tell you. Off-limits," he said. "But it really gets you going. I understand where he's coming from when he makes those comments. Some people say, 'Wow, what was that all about?' But when you know from before and you start getting to know him, you know how he means it."

In other words, somewhere along the way, you come to realize his F-bombs are terms of endearment, as is any suggestion during particularly bad meetings that the entire team would be better off if it disbanded.

Guillen's first meeting of the 2011 season had produced fruit—at least for a little while. The season had started well. Isn't that the kind of thing people say when they begin telling a horrible story? It's like a newspaper story that begins, "Neighbors described him as quiet."

It *had* started out well and with such unbridled optimism. The Sox won six of their first nine games. Their season started out so well that Tampa Bay held a players-only meeting six games into the season after losing a game in Chicago 5–1.

The Sox went downhill shortly after. The Rays? They went 9–3 over their next twelve games and would eventually win the American League wild card.

Even during the White Sox' horrendous first two months of the 2011 season, Guillen did not call a team meeting to ream out his troops. The absence of one was meant to send a message to the players: *What has happened here is a bizarre aberration that eventually will be righted later in the season. We will not dignify its existence with a team meeting.*

Or, as Ozzie might have put it: A team meeting? Fuck that.

Whether the approach was the reason the Sox eventually turned things around is open for debate.

Most of the time, baseball seasons do not turn around immediately because of one meeting. Confidence is not conferred on a team in one session. It builds little by little, with the manager trying to coax it out of his players. Guillen is a combination of cheerleader and realist.

On the one hand, he tells them that they are on their own. On the other, he tells them they have no bigger fan than him. It sounds like a mixed message but it's not. He's with them all the way, but they're the ones who will decide the outcome of games and seasons.

For Ozzie, any discussion of the relative importance of players versus coaches in sports invariably leads to Phil Jackson. The argument that Jackson was a great coach simply because his teams won eleven NBA titles is one that brings the White Sox manager to the edge of insanity. Players, not coaches, win titles, Guillen insists. By his way of thinking, Jackson won titles because of Michael Jordan and Scottie Pippen in Chicago, and because of Shaquille O'Neal and Kobe Bryant in Los Angeles. It's a way of thinking that's hard to derail.

Again, Guillen says, nothing personal. But the idea that Jackson's Zen-master approach to running a team and dealing with players suddenly turned Jordan into a champion is where Ozzie draws the line.

"Let's see Phil win in New Jersey," he said.

His point is that no coach or manager, himself included, can win without talent. It's not a radical idea, but it seems to be to those who belong to the Cult of the Coach. They're the ones who believe that every *X* and every *O* is a stroke of genius. They're the ones who believe that every call to the bullpen by the manager is a voice from heaven.

A baseball manager certainly isn't going to win without talented players on his roster. There's nowhere to hide in a 162-game season. There's no stealth strategy that's going to surprise opponents and hide deficiencies over the long term. Jackson was adept at getting superstars to coexist, no easy accomplishment. He showed a knack for pushing the right emotional buttons with Bryant, challenging him in ways other coaches might not have. It worked. But, again, if his best player had been, say, Luke Walton, it wouldn't have mattered what buttons or how many buttons he pushed.

Two months into the 2011 season, Guillen managed his 1,200th career game. For all the work he had put in, and for all the amateur psychology he had dabbled in to get his players to perform better, he knew why he had lasted so long.

"The only reason I'm still here is because Kenny gave me good players in the past, and he gave me good players in the present," he said. "If they give you bad players, you'll get fired. I think Kenny and Jerry and Rick [Hahn, the Sox' assistant general manager] put a good ball club together, made me compete. That's the only reason you survive. There's no manager with a losing career. They don't last too long. The only reason they don't last too long is because the players they have can't compete."

Midway through the 2011 season, only four other managers had been with their teams as long as the eight years Guillen had been with the White Sox—Tony La Russa (sixteen), the Angels' Mike Scioscia (twelve), the Twins' Ron Gardenhire (ten), and the Red Sox' Terry Francona (eight).

Guillen walked away from the White Sox two games before the season ended, and the Red Sox declined to pick up Francona's option after the team's spectacular collapse. That's how it works in baseball. If the White Sox had won in 2011, Reinsdorf might have given Guillen that contract extension. But they didn't. And Francona likely would still be the Red Sox manager if the team had made the playoffs. But they didn't. The players sealed their managers' fates.

Ozzie knows what bad teams look like. He played on a few of them. In 2000, in his final season as a player, the Devil Rays lost ninety-two games. So did the 1989 White Sox team he played on, which finished 29½ games out of first place.

John McGraw wouldn't have been able to win with either team.

Early on in 2011, Guillen's biggest challenge was to let his team know it would never be mistaken for those teams. No matter how bad things got, there was too much talent on the White Sox' roster for the club to be god-awful. Average, mediocre, disappointing? Absolutely. But god-awful? No.

Whether Jeffrey Loria signs on for a talent upgrade year after year in Miami will determine whether Guillen gives similar verbal encouragement to the Marlins or complains publicly about the payroll.

"I know how that feels when you come to the ballpark and you know you're going to lose," he said during the 2011 season. "I know that feeling. [White Sox players] don't know that feeling yet. They're lucky to be playing for a good team. They haven't played for a bad team yet. I played for a lot of bad teams. I know it's no fun coming to the ballpark and saying, 'Oh, boy, who's pitching today? We're down by seven runs in the first inning. I know it's going to happen.' We don't have that now. I know it's up to the players. We've got to dig in. We've got to fight."

So he stayed the course. He kept an eye out for players who dared to make the fatal mistake of wallowing in self-pity. If they thought somebody in the stands was going to feel sorry for them, they were wrong. They were alone. They needed to know this for their own good. He could make them feel better, or a sports shrink could make them feel better, but only the strongest would survive. He would reward the struggling team by striking the pose of the confident skipper, unburdened by the worries of today, knowing that tomorrow was going to be the day when everything changed for the better.

And when the grumbling outside the team became too loud to ignore, he would talk again (and again) about taking full responsibility for the failings of his ball club. And if that meant he could get fired, well, he would talk all day about that—though he might not be able to stop himself from mentioning that, the last he looked, he didn't hit the ball, catch the ball, or throw the ball.

On August 29, with his team's record a discouraging 67–66, Guillen went off on a jag about being totally accountable for his team's failings. Blame me, he said, don't blame the players. Before critics could blame him, he had already blamed himself, making it a kind of preemptive blame.

But when asked what he would have done differently, with the luxury of hindsight, he said he wouldn't have changed a thing. In essence, then, he really wasn't taking the blame. He was absorbing the abuse so that others wouldn't have to, but he didn't really believe the abuse was warranted.

"I'm not hiding from anybody," he said. "They want to blame me, I blame myself. Listen, in 2007 we had a very a bad team [a 72–90 record]. I didn't blame anybody. I blamed myself. If people thought we were going to win with that team . . . the next year, there were twelve players from that roster who weren't on any big-league team. And I said, 'Blame me.' I don't mind."

Now what would a psychologist say about a man who takes responsibility with a wink? Probably that the man would prefer to talk about the general manager who had put the 2007 roster together.

A day later, Guillen made public his desire for a contract

extension. He might have been willing to take the blame for the disappointing season to that point, but he was not willing to go through another year without some proof that he was wanted.

Did it stem from his need for the stability he lacked as a child? Is that what a mental-health expert would say about Guillen? Perhaps. Ozzie would probably say he needed more money for vodka and Budweiser.

·5·

BE NURTURING, NO MATTER HOW MUCH IT HURTS

One by one, the boys and girls approached the manager, climbed onto his lap as if he were Santa Claus, and smiled their frozen smiles for the person taking the photos.

It was Christmas in July for Ozzie.

"How you doing, man?" he said, greeting each of them with a big grin and a high five.

This was during the break for the 2011 All-Star Game. While most everyone else in baseball was trying to get away from it all after the long grind of the first half of the season, Guillen was happily settled in at a skills camp in suburban Chicago for kids aged seven to eleven.

"We're going to have some fun," he told them, and for the next three hours, they had the distinction of having the manager of a major-league team throw ground balls and batting practice to them.

He was in his element, goofing around with young ballplayers whose parents had spent $225 each for this hands-on experience. And the kids immediately took to him. One player fired a ball to him from close range, and Ozzie, in mock anger, asked whether the boy was trying to kill him.

"I'm going to pitch to you, and I'm going to strike you out!" the manager said.

This day wasn't so different from any day with Guillen in the Sox clubhouse, except for the absence of F-bombs—though you had the distinct feeling that if these sessions went just a tad longer, there would be no holding back the four-lettered floodwaters.

He had no plans to watch the All-Star Game on TV the next day, even though Paul Konerko and Carlos Quentin would be playing. He needed to recharge his batteries. He needed time away from his up-and-down team, from slumping hitters, from any players who might be a bit too self-absorbed.

He needed time with kids who had no agendas.

"I want to be the catcher because I'm wearing a cup," one boy announced.

Wow. Ballplayers and their demands these days.

Guillen takes pride in how he deals with young professional players. He doesn't treat them as if they are delicate packages. He treats them with a combination of trust and tough love.

He had been painted as an obstructionist when it came to Dayan Viciedo, which, in a way, he was. He didn't want to have to push a veteran out of the lineup to make way for a rookie. As a rule, he has no use for players in the minor leagues, simply because they can't do a thing for him in the present. It's not personal. But once a minor leaguer lands with the big club, Guillen will make him feel as if he belongs. It's one of the things he does best as a manager. He has shown a deft touch with young players struggling with confidence in what often is a brutal profession.

Jon Garland was one of them. No one denied the kid's ability when he got to the big leagues as a twenty-year-old pitcher in 2000. But he couldn't seem to break through the ceiling that White Sox manager Jerry Manuel had constructed for him. He'd get through the fifth inning and know that, no matter how well he was pitching, Manuel likely was going to replace him with a reliever.

Garland was starving for more. He knew there was a very good chance he would take a beating, but he figured if he got it out of the way when he was twenty-one or twenty-two, he'd be that much better later. Manuel wouldn't budge. Because of it, anything beyond five innings started to look like Mount Everest to Garland. It wasn't until Ozzie arrived in 2004 that things changed. And they changed immediately.

"I didn't care how they had treated him before," Guillen said. "I just worried about how I treated him. I wasn't going to say, 'I'm going to treat you better because the other manager treated you like shit.' No, no, no. I will treat you the way I think you should be treated. I'm going to give you the opportunity."

In his first start under Guillen, Garland pitched eight innings and allowed four hits and one run in a road victory against the Yankees. Two years earlier, in Garland's first start of the 2002 season, Manuel had pulled him after five innings and ninety-three pitches during a 5–2 loss in Kansas City. Guillen believes that pain is part of the process of learning and that trying to numb a player to it only hurts him in the end.

"He lets you stay out there and learn," said Garland, who played for the Los Angeles Dodgers in 2011. "He gives you an opportunity to get that time under your belt. He lets you learn, one way or the other, good or bad. Coming to the big leagues, you're going to have to go through those experiences to learn how to succeed at that level. You're going to have to fail. You'll have to be stuck in a tough situation. He basically gives you that opportunity right away. He doesn't make you earn it. I think a lot of that is, he realizes that those things need to happen for you to progress as a big leaguer."

In his first four years with the White Sox, Garland threw one complete game. In the next four years under Guillen, he had seven.

In Manuel's defense, his approach to Garland was in line with how a lot of managers deal with young pitchers. He wanted to ease Garland into the big leagues and, by doing so, protect him. Some young players get their self-esteem crushed early and never recover.

"That definitely could have been part of their plan with a young guy," Garland said. "I've been on teams with a Max Scherzer or a Mat Latos, young guys coming up where they don't want to put too much of a burden on them right away and kind of damage their arm or damage them as a player right away. That could have been for my benefit. I don't know. Maybe there was nothing there, and my style of pitching at the time scared them a little, and they figured those were moves they needed to make."

But what's the expiration date on protecting young players? For Garland, the act of being protected for so long ate at his confidence. Why didn't Manuel trust him enough to keep him on the mound? And how was Garland supposed to learn how to pitch late into games if his manager rarely gave him the chance? It was a pitcher's catch-22.

For managers with a quick hook, self-preservation is involved. They're not going to put themselves in a position to lose games just to make a rookie feel good.

As it turned out, the cautious approach might have hurt Manuel. Garland went 18–10 in 2005, Guillen's second season, and was an All-Star. Oh, yeah, and the Sox won the World Series that year, with Garland pitching a complete-game four-hitter in the American League Championship Series and getting a no-decision in the Sox' sweep of the Astros in the Fall Classic.

He went 18–7 in 2006. His best year under Manuel was 12–12.

"My overall confidence increased after Ozzie's first year," Garland said. "The next year going out there starting a game, you knew it was your game to finish, if you could. Just the confidence going into the game that he was going to allow you to do that made me a better pitcher."

It's not exactly a sink-or-swim approach. That would imply a certain coldness on Guillen's part. He won't let young players drown. He will, however, let them swallow a few gulps of water before he rescues them. The key is to not make them feel worse after they do struggle. Build up, rather than tear down.

"Garland got the ball," Guillen said. "Here, pitch. Seven innings. You struggle? Nobody's in the bullpen warming up. See what happens.

"Joe Crede. Aaron Rowand. Juan Uribe. Beckham. All those guys struggled. Well, if you kick them in the ass, then they have no confidence in themselves. Even with older players like Dunn and Rios, I told them, 'Man, let's go out and play and see what happens.'

"You have to have fucking confidence and blame yourself as the manager, take the responsibility if those guys fail. But I'd rather see the kid fail early in his career to learn."

In his natural state, a yapping, enthusiastic Ozzie Guillen greets White Sox first baseman Paul Konerko after a home run. Players know he's on their side—as long as they play hard. *(Photo courtesy of* Chicago Sun-Times. *Reprinted with permission.)*

Ozzie makes a point in his old office at U.S. Cellular Field in Chicago. He's always making a point, whether it's welcomed or not. *(Photo courtesy of* Chicago Sun-Times. *Reprinted with permission.)*

Many managers consider daily sessions with the media a chore; Ozzie thinks of them as wonderful opportunities to sound off on anything and everything in front of a captive audience. *(Photo courtesy of* Chicago Sun-Times. *Reprinted with permission.)*

In 2006, three months after winning the World Series, the Venezuelan-born Ozzie is sworn in as a U.S. citizen, along with his wife, Ibis, and his middle child, Oney. Oney is the son most like his father, which may be why his tongue has gotten him into trouble. *(Photo courtesy of* Chicago Sun-Times. *Reprinted with permission.)*

The oldest of Guillen's three sons, Ozzie Jr. worked as a radio sports talk show host in Chicago and as a radio announcer for the White Sox' Spanish broadcasts. *(Photo courtesy of* Chicago Sun-Times. *Reprinted with permission.)*

Ozzie fumed after the White Sox waited until the twenty-second round of the 2010 MLB draft to select his youngest son, Ozney. It played a part in the falling out between Guillen and general manager Kenny Williams. *(Photo by Joe Robbins/Getty Images)*

Ozzie having a "discussion" with umpire Joe West. Guillen says West too often wants to be the center of attention but respects him nonetheless. *(Photo courtesy of* Chicago Sun-Times. *Reprinted with permission.)*

In a not uncommon occurrence, Ozzie gets tossed from a game, with catcher A. J. Pierzynski as a witness. Guillen will stand up for his players, but he says getting ejected rarely helps his team. *(Photo courtesy of* Chicago Sun-Times. *Reprinted with permission.)*

In a happier time with general manager Kenny Williams, Ozzie holds up his jersey on November 3, 2003, the day the White Sox hired him as manager. *(Photo courtesy of* Chicago Sun-Times. *Reprinted with permission.)*

In the biggest moment of his career, Ozzie raises the World Series trophy in 2005 after the Sox swept the Houston Astros. The team went 11-1 in the postseason that year. *(Photo courtesy of* Chicago Sun-Times. *Reprinted with permission.)*

Guillen wanted an extremely focused Paul Konerko to relax about hitting but finally realized it was an unrealistic request. Konerko taught him that every player is different and that a manager shouldn't presume to know what goes through a player's mind. *(Photo courtesy of* Chicago Sun-Times. *Reprinted with permission.)*

In the face of constant fan pressure to make a change, Ozzie stood by slugger Adam Dunn for most of the 2011 season. His loyalty wasn't rewarded; Dunn hit .159 and struck out 177 times. *(Photo courtesy of* Chicago Sun-Times. *Reprinted with permission.)*

There was also pressure to bench a slumping Juan Pierre, but Ozzie had deep respect for him and was worried that if he sat the outfielder, he would lose the rest of the team. Pierre ended up hitting .279 and living up to Guillen's belief in him. *(Photo courtesy of* Chicago Sun-Times. *Reprinted with permission.)*

Ozzie refused to insert the forty-three-year-old shortstop Omar Vizquel into a lopsided game in 2011, viewing it as an insult to a future Hall of Famer. Guillen drew on his own unhappy experience as a veteran player who was sent into a game in the late innings of a blowout. *(Photo courtesy of* Chicago Sun-Times. *Reprinted with permission.)*

A young Ozzie Guillen in a throwback White Sox uniform at old Comiskey Park in the 1980s, where he learned valuable, sometimes painful lessons from veteran teammates like Carlton Fisk and Tom Seaver. *(Photo courtesy of* Chicago Sun-Times. *Reprinted with permission.)*

Ozzie, a talented shortstop, turns a double play against the Seattle Mariners and a hard-charging Joey Cora. Cora would go on to serve as Guillen's bench coach in Chicago and Miami. *(Photo courtesy of* Chicago Sun-Times. *Reprinted with permission.)*

Ozzie and ESPN baseball analyst John Kruk were minor-league teammates for three years, with Kruk playing a big role in teaching the young Venezuelan about life in the United States. He takes the credit—and the blame—for Guillen's salty language. Here, they chat during spring training in 2011.

Ozzie talking with, from left, White Sox chairman Jerry Reinsdorf, St. Louis Cardinals manager Tony La Russa, and Sox vice chairman Eddie Einhorn. La Russa was Guillen's first big-league manager, in 1985 in Chicago. *(Photo courtesy of* Chicago Sun-Times. *Reprinted with permission.)*

Ozzie takes a breather during the 2011 All-Star break by working with kids at a summer skills camp. He's very good at nurturing young big leaguers, as well. *(Photo courtesy of* Chicago Sun-Times. *Reprinted with permission.)*

Ozzie is all smiles as he is introduced as the Miami Marlins' new manager on September 28, 2011. Marlins owner Jeffrey Loria, right, says he's not worried that the outspoken Guillen might ruffle feathers. That's good, because Ozzie surely will. *(Walter Michot/*Miami Herald*/MCT via Getty Images)*

Guillen had seen plenty of young teammates fail and go on to long, productive careers. Robin Ventura went through an 0-for-41 slump during his rookie year in 1990. Frank Thomas had struggled at times.

The attention Guillen gives to rookies isn't just part of a managerial philosophy he devised while sitting in a one-man think tank. He was that way as a player. He often would take younger teammates aside. He did it in 1995, his eleventh season in the majors, with Ray Durham, who was a twenty-three-year-old rookie second baseman.

"In spring training, I heard somebody instructing Durham on how to play second base," said Joe Goddard, who was covering the Sox that year for the *Chicago Sun-Times*. "So I sat under a tree in Sarasota, and I watched a shortstop showing a second baseman how to play his position. It went on for a half an hour. That's the first time I realized that Ozzie was exceptional, not just as a player but as an instructor.

"Ozzie didn't ask permission. He just said, 'Come with me,' and they went out to this field. It didn't surprise me too much when Ozzie got the Sox managing job."

Guillen shrugs. That's how it is. He's not going to say a word to a veteran like Matt Thornton after a bad performance. But he'd reassure Sergio Santos or Chris Sale in a similar situation to make sure their self-worth doesn't end up looking like the remains of a dropped lightbulb. He'll do the same thing in Miami with Logan Morrison and the other young players.

It's what he did with Bobby Jenks after Game 2 of the 2005 World Series. Jenks had blown a save, giving up two runs in the ninth inning of a game the Sox ended up winning. Guillen wanted Jenks to know that he believed in him. He wanted

Jenks to know that if the world suddenly began crumbling, his belief in his closer would not run and seek shelter immediately. It's the kind of stubborn faith that sometimes drove Sox fans crazy, but it's a faith that keeps the pilot light burning for a lot of young, vulnerable players.

"This is the World Series, and this is a kid," Guillen said. "The first thing I did was hug him and say, 'Hey, don't worry about it. Just be ready tomorrow. You're going to be the guy tomorrow.' If that had happened to a veteran or someone who was in that situation before, maybe I would have handled it a different way."

And Jenks did get the ball the next game, throwing two scoreless innings in the Sox' fourteen-inning victory over Houston.

That was vintage Ozzie, showing trust and having patience. Trust and patience are easy to talk about but harder to execute, especially when events head in a southerly direction. It's a difficult concept for a manager to embrace in a business that prefers its gratification to be of the instant kind. Guillen's outlook is long-term and direct: be nurturing, no matter how much it hurts.

"And don't kick them in the ass when they struggle," he said. "Teach them and make sure you help them. A lot of managers see you're not playing well, they turn their back on you, they don't want to see you, they try to avoid you. That's the player you have to talk to, you have to teach.

"Everybody that comes to the big leagues doesn't have experience. They don't know what's going on here. I think that's one of the reasons you have to help those guys to reach their potential. Teaching them how to play the game right. Teaching them how to survive. Teaching them to be tough.

Teaching them to respect. You want to teach them how to go about your business in the big leagues.

"You throw a hundred innings in the minor leagues, that's like sixty innings in the big leagues because mentally and physically, it's harder. You have to deal with that and you have to help those guys the best you can. Because when they grow up, they will appreciate that."

In 2004, his first season as a big-league manager, Guillen made a conscious effort to support young players on the roster. It became one of his guiding principles. He'd chat with them on flights as the Sox crisscrossed the country. He'd include them in conversations during many of his excursions into the clubhouse.

He was a rookie, too, a forty-year-old first-time manager making his way through a new world. He started doing things that other managers wouldn't. It was his presence in the clubhouse that took some getting used to by his team.

Guillen has never lost the feeling of being a player, and it's probably not going too far to say that he still considers himself one when he looks in the mirror. He's constantly changing his facial hair, the way baseball players tend to do. Today a goatee, next week a mustache, the week after that who knows?

The clubhouse is supposed to be the domain of the players. It's their sanctuary. If problems crop up in the clubhouse, tradition demands that the players take care of it themselves. They're supposed to do the policing. To see Guillen there so often was an eye-opener even for the younger players, who had been brought up on the idea, passed down from baseball generation to baseball generation, that managers are supposed to keep their distance.

"To an extent, he does still realize that the players' clubhouse is the players' clubhouse," Garland said. "But he wanted to be in the mix. He still wanted to be in the game, so he was in there. I think a lot of managers have that understanding of, it's the team's clubhouse. That's where the players come together. That's where they do their thing. But some managers are still around just to catch a vibe to see how the team's doing, to see how guys are doing, to stay in tune with their team."

Most don't linger the way Guillen does. When Lou Piniella was the manager of the Cubs, he was a stranger in a strange land whenever he walked from his office through the clubhouse on his way to the dugout. He didn't stop often. Most managers are like that.

Guillen gets away with being different because, well, he *is* different. Garland sees that now after stops with four other teams.

"He has a great understanding that he's only going to be as good as the team," he said. "There have been a few teams I've been on where it seems like the manager thought that he could make the team better by doing certain things. I think Ozzie has the understanding that, 'Look, we prepare them, and now they're either going to go out there and make us look good or look bad.' He didn't add any pressure to any of the players. He wasn't a stickler, always on guys about little things. . . . It relaxed us."

Guillen sounds like a proud teacher when he talks about former players who have gone on to other teams and succeeded. And it's not even the success so much that gets him excited. It's the way the players approach the game, the way they carry themselves. If you hustle and play with intelligence, Ozzie will love you forever, even if you're not wearing a White Sox or Marlins uniform anymore.

"All my players who go on to somewhere else, they know how to play the game," he said. "They know how to approach it. They know how to compete. That's all I care [about]."

In his mind, those are the players who will win a manager a lot of baseball games. To see them go from wide-eyed, adrift young ballplayers to unflappable veterans might be Guillen's biggest reward in baseball. The rest isn't exactly boring. It's just not as interesting. It's certainly not as challenging.

"It's easy when you're a manager and the guy is hitting .350," he said. "How about the guy hitting .120? That's the guy who needs you the most. I think my coaching staff and myself, we're pretty good about that. We don't kick people in the gut and send them away. . . . Give them the opportunity, they grab it, they play good, and they come out good players."

In his second year, the White Sox came out world champions. And Ozzie, the constant gardener who had watered, weeded, and nurtured, enjoyed watching his players sprout.

The explosions, the laughs, the vulgarity—that's Ozzie. But so is this. In early September 2011, the Sox lost a road game to the Detroit Tigers and their ace pitcher Justin Verlander. Afterward, outside the clubhouse, Guillen saw his wife with tears in her eyes. Concerned, he rushed over to her. Had something happened at home?

No. The woman she was standing with was Kerry Lindsay, the mother of Shane Lindsay, an Australian relief pitcher who had made his major-league debut that night. When she found out that the Sox were calling up her son from Triple-A, she bought a plane ticket for $4,000 and flew from Melbourne to Detroit. It took her twenty-four hours, but she made it in time to see her son pitch an inning of relief.

"Believe me, I don't get too sensitive about too much stuff, and that one made me forget how bad we played," Guillen said. "Right away, it made me forget. It was a great thing that happened to us, at least to me. . . . There is nothing better than when your kids have success. That's one of the biggest thrills you can have as a parent."

When Guillen joined the Florida Marlins as a third-base coach in 2002, the team was getting ready to release shortstop Alex Gonzalez. Gonzalez had been an All-Star in 1999, his first full season in the majors, but he had been a huge disappointment the two seasons afterward. Baseball teams aren't in the habit of waiting for players to come around, particularly players with a reputation for not working hard.

The new manager, Jeff Torborg, didn't feel as if he had a good read on the enigmatic shortstop, and before the organization did anything rash he wanted another opinion. So he called Ozzie, who had been known to have opinions.

"Do you know him?" Torborg said.

"Gonzalez is the best shortstop in baseball," Guillen said flatly.

"What?!"

"Yes. Not just the National League. Not just the American League."

"Is he better than Vizquel?" Torborg said.

"Yes, he's better than Vizquel."

For Guillen to rate Alex Gonzalez ahead of Omar Vizquel might have been considered heresy in Venezuela, where all three had been raised. The royal bloodline of Venezuelan shortstops went from Chico Carrasquel to Luis Aparicio to Dave Concepcion to Guillen to Vizquel. For Guillen to put Gonzalez over Vizquel seemed to be crazy talk, if not a national scandal. Vizquel already had won nine Gold Gloves at that point, Gonzalez none.

"Why do they want to release him?" Torborg said.

"Because he's a dog. That's why they want to release him. Let me have a chance."

Ozzie saw a kid who had fielding skills that few players possessed. He also saw a kid who didn't run the bases hard. Even then, it was a failing he couldn't abide.

Guillen distinctly remembered a 1999 game against the Marlins when he was playing for the Atlanta Braves. Someone had hit a fly ball toward short left field, and Gonzalez ran after it with all the seriousness of a child chasing soap bubbles. Even the Braves were offended by the Florida shortstop's lack of hustle.

"People in our dugout said, 'Next fucking time he comes to the plate, hit his ass,'" Guillen said. "John Smoltz was pitching for us. Here comes Gonzalez. And Smoltz drilled his ass. Boom! Play the fucking game right."

So three years later, here was Guillen presented with that same player. All he asked from Torborg was one year. Just give him one year with Gonzalez to see if he could get him to be the player he had been in 1999, his All-Star year.

We'll see, Torborg said.

When Guillen arrived at spring training, he was informed that the rookie Miguel Cabrera would be playing shortstop. Cabrera also was from Venezuela, and of all the things Guillen knew about him, the most important was that he wasn't a shortstop.

"I said, 'Wait a minute, Cabrera's a what?'" Guillen said. "Yeah, he's a shortstop—at Single-A or goddamn rookie league. He's not a fucking big-league shortstop.

"I told Jeff, 'Listen, when you see this kid, you tell me if he's a shortstop or not.' He saw Cabrera for the first time. He was like, 'Holy shit!' I said, 'I told you he wasn't a shortstop.' He was twenty years old. He was like six-three, three hundred pounds. He's not a shortstop."

Guillen had already cornered Gonzalez. There was a lot riding on how the shortstop played and carried himself in 2002, not the least of which was Guillen's own reputation. He had gone to bat for Gonzalez. But Ozzie also saw a chance for the Marlins to do some damage in the National League East.

"Gonzalez comes into spring training," Guillen said. "I grab him, sit down with him. The general manager [Larry Beinfest] was there. I said, 'Listen, motherfucker, you keep playing the fucking way you've been playing, you're going to be in fucking Triple-A for the rest of your fucking life. You pull that shit with us, you're not playing with this team.' That's what he needed. He knew I wasn't going to put up with that shit."

Gonzalez played in only forty-two games that season because of a dislocated shoulder. But Guillen had seen enough to know that the Marlins had a committed shortstop.

The next year, he hit eighteen home runs and had seventy-seven runs batted in, his best numbers to that point in his career. He also had the fewest errors to that point as a big leaguer.

The 2003 Marlins, who got into the playoffs with a wild-card berth, seemed to find themselves after Jack McKeon replaced Torborg as manager in May. They beat the San Francisco Giants in a first-round playoff series. They were five outs away from being knocked out of the National League Championship Series before coming back and stunning the

Chicago Cubs. Then they mowed down the New York Yankees in the World Series.

"It was the best infield I saw in my life—*my life*," Guillen said. "For two years. Wow. It was fun to watch that shit. Best infield I've ever seen by a lot. Mike Lowell at third, Gonzalez at short, Luis Castillo at second, and Derrek Lee at first."

And Cabrera? He was called up from the minors during the season and played a key role for the Marlins in the playoffs—as an outfielder.

Now let's see what Guillen can do with Miami infielder Hanley Ramirez, an expensive, underperforming, sometimes disruptive player. Or with Carlos Zambrano, the fiery and explosive pitcher who came over to the Marlins from the Chicago Cubs and whose tantrums and erratic behavior have become the stuff of legend.

Guillen loves saying that he predicted something before it actually happened. Absolutely loves it. When the White Sox opened the 2011 season in Cleveland, he predicted that the Indians would be in the thick of the race in the American League Central, even though most prognosticators had them finishing low in the division. They finished second. As the season went along, whenever someone asked him about the Tribe, Guillen would remind everyone that a certain manager wearing a White Sox uniform had said Cleveland would be good.

He didn't exactly see the future when it came to Brent Morel, but one of his sons did. And in Ozzie's world, that's just as good.

In 2008, Oney Guillen and Morel played for the Sox' Single-A affiliate in Kannapolis, North Carolina.

"You know who told me the kid's going to be in the big leagues? Oney," he said. "Oney was his teammate with Beckham. I went out to see Oney there, and he said, 'Dad, this guy is going to play third base for you very soon.' I said, 'This kid? He just signed.' He said, 'You watch.' He was his roommate and saw him play all the time. Oney taught him everything he knows—off the field."

Morel had been drafted the same year as the outgoing Gordon Beckham, who would zip through the minors in 2008 and be called up to the big-league team in June 2009. Morel's path to Chicago was slower and more deliberate, which suited his personality. He was a September call-up in 2010, then made the team coming out of spring training in 2011.

Armed with his son's scouting report, Ozzie kept an eye on the kid. In a game in July, Morel hadn't run the bases with the kind of effort required at the major-league level, at least in Guillen's view. It was the dreaded Lack of Effort, and Guillen was waiting for him at the dugout steps. Morel, he said, would find himself back in Triple-A—"fucking Charlotte"—if that ever happened again.

How did Morel react?

"Like he had been shot in the fucking head," Guillen said later. "I told Joey [Cora], 'You better tell him what I think about him right now.' Why? Because some people think they're doing a good thing, and they're not. They think, 'Oh, I'm doing pretty good.' In my eyes, no, you're not. I'm going to let you know about what's going on."

Morel said he thought he had been running hard. That's what a manager is sometimes there for: to tell you that the image you have of yourself is seriously misguided.

Guillen's reputation, inside and outside of baseball, is that of a loud, loose, joyful, and impetuous man who happens to be a manager. Much of it is accurate; some isn't. Nowhere in that view of him is an adjective that also fits: demanding. He learned it from his first major-league manager, a guy not given to smiling. When Guillen came to the Sox as a yapping twenty-one-year-old in 1985, Tony La Russa was running the show.

"Having Tony as a manager in his rookie year helped him a lot," said his oldest son, Ozzie Jr. "Tony was hard on him to play the game the right way. Run the bases hard. Be a pro. My dad thinks that when you're young those are the most important years because that's how you're going to come out."

Which is why he had been hard on Morel, even for a brief moment. The White Sox had brought him up to the big leagues because his fielding was excellent. He could make the sensational plays, and he could make the routine plays. Many times, it's the routine plays, the day-to-day, garden-variety grounders, that separate the players from the frauds. Morel was as consistent as a metronome, and Guillen liked that about him.

He had sat down with the rookie early in the season. Morel had been discouraged because his batting average was hovering around the .200 mark. But the plan for the season had never been for him to hit .280. The plan was for everybody else in the starting lineup to hit consistently. Dunn and Rios weren't cooperating.

So now Morel was in Ozzie's office.

"Don't worry about it," Guillen said. "Nobody's hitting, except for Carlos [Quentin] and PK [Konerko]. Obviously, you're a rookie. Every at-bat means a lot to you. It has to be the opposite. You've got to relax and get good at-bats, and good things are going to happen."

Morel walked out with mixed emotions. It felt good to know that the manager was on his side and was rooting for him.

But even though the club didn't have lofty expectations for him as a hitter, he wanted to contribute at the plate. He didn't want to be seen as a one-dimensional player.

Guillen hadn't taken his own offensive skills too seriously when he played, and he wanted to inject some of that devil-may-care attitude into the kid. Morel understood why the manager was doing it. He wanted to make life as easy as he could for him.

"I feel like I'm getting a decent amount of playing time," he said. "When I'm not playing good, I'm not in the lineup. There's not too much pressure on me. He wants me to go out there and just play some good D and just kind of let it happen. He does a good job trying to take the pressure off me. . . . As much as people say, 'Don't worry about this, don't worry about that,' it's still something I want to do for myself and the team. I have my own expectations."

Guillen prides himself on showing confidence in young players by throwing them into the fire, but he's smart enough to know that third-degree burns don't do anybody any good. Most times when the White Sox were facing a particularly tough right-handed pitcher, Guillen would insert Omar Vizquel or, early in the season, Mark Teahen into the lineup and give Morel the day off.

Morel was in the lineup the first two times the Sox faced Verlander, a right-hander with enough strength and endurance to make veteran hitters consider a career change. Morel went 1-for-6 with no strikeouts combined in those two games, which is a kind of success story in that he hadn't needed a psychologist's couch afterward. But when the Sox faced Verlander twice in July, Guillen sat Morel. It was better that way.

On July 26, Verlander struck out Konerko with a 100-mph

fastball, his hardest thrown ball of the night. It came on his 120th pitch. That's horror-flick stuff. You put a rookie in that spot, and you might need a forklift truck to get him back to the dugout. Guillen knew this. It's a balancing act between showing faith and keeping a kid's hands away from the lion's cage.

Ozzie couldn't do anything about Morel's unplugged power numbers. Through August, he had hit just two home runs, the kind of production normally associated with a second baseman or a field-goal kicker. But he was hitting .251, and that was good enough for Guillen.

"He's done what we think he can do," he said. "Our offense has been so bad that it doesn't look like the guy contributes, but yes he does. When the season started, I would have taken .250, .260, out of him, and he plays the way he plays third base. People say, 'Oh, look at what kind of year he's had,' because we're not hitting. I think he contributes more than people think, and I'm very happy that he's playing the way he's playing right now."

What bothered Guillen was Morel's mellow demeanor. It would be one thing if Morel changed into tights and a cape in a phone booth before going on the diamond. But he was mild-mannered on and off the field—too mild-mannered for Ozzie's tastes. He preferred boisterousness in his players. Guillen would look at Morel and sigh, as if to say, "What's a manager to do?"

"I've played this way my whole life, so I don't think he's going to try to change me," Morel said. "He just wants me to produce and help the team win. However I am, I think he's fine with it."

Seemingly out of nowhere, Morel hit eight home runs in September. Guillen wouldn't take any credit for that. The kid deserved it. So did Walker, the hitting coach. But Guillen deserved a bow for his patience and for not trying to push a personality transplant on the kid.

As long as you play the game the right way, Ozzie will be okay with you. You can have the ugliest swing in baseball history, but if you play hard, he's fine with you. If you're on his team and happen to be young, you have a target on your back, the good kind.

"I'm going to raise you the way people should be raised," he said. "Look at the kids I raised: Gavin Floyd, John Danks, the Missile [Alexei Ramirez], Jon Garland, Juan Uribe. They play the game right. Why? Because they grow up with us. I don't care if you're horseshit, play the game right."

For all his success with bringing along young talent, Guillen took his time in embracing Brent Lillibridge. Early in the 2011 season, whenever there was a group of reporters around Lillibridge and Guillen happened to be walking by, the skipper would grumble under his breath. He knew what people were saying on the radio talk shows: Why wasn't Lillibridge playing more? Clearly, he was a great fielder. He had made a game-ending diving catch on Robinson Cano's screaming line drive to right field to preserve a 3–2 victory over the Yankees in late April. Earlier in the same inning, he had banged into the wall while making a catch of a long Alex Rodriguez fly ball. He was all over ESPN's *SportsCenter* that day and at various points of the season for similar breathtaking defensive plays.

The problem with Lillibridge wasn't fielding. It was a lack of consistency at the plate. He had played parts of three major-league seasons, starting in 2008 with the Atlanta Braves before moving to the White Sox organization the next year. It was the same thing every season. He couldn't seem to put together a string of games in which he played well. It's why he had bounced between the minors and the majors the previous three years.

But 2011 was different. He was on the big-league club for good and had shown he was capable of playing several different positions. With the Sox struggling in the standings, the background noise insisting that he deserved a shot grew louder and louder. Guillen was frustrated by it. Hadn't people been paying attention? Nothing against Lillibridge, but hadn't fans and media noticed his inconsistency at the plate?

All the love for the twenty-seven-year-old outfielder was getting under Ozzie's skin. Lillibridge didn't look like an everyday player to him.

After one game on the road, Ozzie and his wife were sitting in a hotel bar. He was looking for a bit of understanding from a trusted companion. He told his wife that Lillibridge was struggling mightily at the plate but that the guy was the best outfielder and the player with the most speed on the team.

"She said, 'If he's so good, why don't you play him every day?'" Guillen said.

Et tu, Ibis?

But Lillibridge kept putting his head down and playing, despite Guillen's insistence that it was too early, that he wasn't ready yet. It was as if he were immune to Ozzie's opinions. In June, he made a leaping catch above the wall in left center field to help John Danks beat Oakland.

"I just told Konerko [that Lillibridge] saved me a bottle of vodka that I won't have to drink tonight," Guillen told reporters afterward.

In August, Lillibridge filled in for an injured Konerko at

first base against Kansas City and made a beautiful pickup of a throw from Morel at third. He had hardly played first base in his life. He also hit a home run to help the Sox beat the Royals.

Guillen couldn't hold out any longer.

"He's starting to turn himself into a pretty good player," he said. "This kid can play every position now. I think he's put himself in a great spot in baseball. Now people find out he can play in the infield and the outfield very good."

But Lillibridge agreed with Guillen's long-held contention that he hadn't been steady enough.

"It's my first full season," he said. "I've played parts of four years, not really showing the consistency of putting together good at-bats every game or even just when I'm in the game. I've got to prove myself now. If I can just be consistent and continue to produce when I'm out there, then I'll get my opportunity, whether it's here or somewhere else. I'm happy as long as I'm in the lineup and contributing. I've got to pay my dues. I've got to show them that I can play a full season and put numbers up and play great defense, and then we'll go from there."

Lillibridge credits God with whatever success he has on the baseball diamond, so he said he didn't care what anybody had to say about how he played the game, including his manager. It's a fine attitude, but in the Sox clubhouse, Guillen's word is the one that carries the ultimate authority. Lillibridge's playing time was in the hands of a much higher power—Ozzie. Then again, with Konerko getting drilled in the calf by a fastball, maybe Guillen and God were working in tandem. Konerko's injury gave Lillibridge the chance to make that play on Morel's throw to first base.

Ozzie's touch hasn't always been golden. When the White Sox sent center fielder Aaron Rowand to the Philadelphia Phillies in a trade that brought Jim Thome to Chicago after the 2005 season, it meant that Guillen was forced to use an outfielder who had played thirteen games in his major-league career. Brian Anderson hit .225 in 2006, and none of Ozzie's cajoling could change the fact that this twenty-four-year-old former first-round draft pick couldn't hit.

In baseball, it's ultimately up to the player. The manager can offer opportunity, advice, and a pep talk, but after that? You might want to start hitting, son. Or start thinking about working for your father-in-law's pool-cleaning business.

Guillen was bothered by suggestions that the White Sox had rushed Beckham to the big leagues before he was ready. He was the eighth pick of the 2008 draft, coming out of the University of Georgia. He played fourteen games of Single-A ball that season. In 2009, he played thirty-eight games for Double-A Birmingham and seventeen games for Triple-A Charlotte before making his debut for the Sox on June 4. It was a surprise Beckham didn't arrive with a bad case of motion sickness.

He hit .270 his rookie year, then spent the next two seasons trying to find himself. He went through a horrendous slump in 2010, his second season in the big leagues. And even though he had bounced back after his come-to-Jesus meeting with Ozzie that year, he struggled mightily at the plate again in 2011.

"We never call anybody too soon," Guillen insisted. "We called him up because he was better than anybody we had. I don't think we call anybody too soon. I never will look in the mirror and say, 'Wow, we called this guy too soon.'"

And yet, Ozzie being Ozzie, he seemed to alter his opinion in late August.

"The expectation was too high," he said. "And we don't let the kid grow up and be a baseball player. I think we, and I include myself, handled it the wrong way. Like, 'Wow, this is the guy.' I wish we handled everyone like Morel."

Why did Ozzie have a change of heart on the topic? Because the Sox had just brought up Dayan Viciedo. Carlos Quentin had hurt his shoulder diving for a line drive and was on the disabled list. There was room for the kid, finally. Guillen had been ripped unmercifully in the press and on talk radio for standing in the way of Viciedo's ascent to the big leagues, but he was right at the most basic level. If fans and media thought a rookie was going to change the team's fortunes, they were crazy.

But Guillen had his conservative cap on now, and he wanted it known that the White Sox had done the right thing by being patient with Viciedo.

In Viciedo's first game, in Seattle, he hit a prodigious three-run homer to lead the Sox to a 9–3 victory over the Mariners. Of course he did. It was in keeping with how the season had gone for Guillen. And now the radio talk shows were on him like sunscreen for not bringing up Viciedo earlier.

"I don't give a shit what people say," Guillen said after the game. "I only give a shit what Jerry Reinsdorf and Kenny Williams say. And people can have their own opinion. That's their job—talk."

While he was at it, Ozzie finally waved a white flag and benched Adam Dunn. He had stood by the bewildered designated hitter longer than most managers would have. For five months, he had witnessed some of the worst hitting the game had seen over an extended period.

"Since spring training, I've been taking a lot of heat from everyone, even from my own family. How long are you going to play him?" he said. "I have no choice. They bring [Viciedo] to play.

"I give [Dunn] a lot of opportunities. You know how many people MF me out there because of him? I don't care. I take it because I'm here for my players. Not for the fans or the people upstairs. I'm here for the players, and I'm going to put the best players out there."

But that was the problem. Dunn wasn't one of the Sox' best players, not even close. Guillen's strength—believing in his people, young and old—had come back to sucker punch him. And now it was on his record for good. Once again, he insisted he wouldn't have changed a thing. If he didn't show faith in his players, where was he? "First place," a chorus of cynics might have chimed in.

Guillen finally said what everybody had been thinking: that the hulking power hitter needed to stay in shape year-round. Dunn was fleshy. He looked more like a hunter who always kept a six-pack handy in the duck blind than a committed ballplayer. But Guillen had backed him until he couldn't anymore. For better or worse, and mostly for the better, this is how Ozzie got to where he is. By believing.

And though Dunn appreciated all the kind words, "that gets me nowhere, other than sanity," he said on the day he was benched. "I don't know how else to handle it. I can take shoelaces out of my shoes, but other than that, that's all I can do."

The players who grew up with Guillen as their manager seem to have the fondest view of him, especially the ones who have gone on to other organizations. They respect his loyalty and his capacity for belief. They appreciate that he remembers what it was like to be a player.

"I would play for him any day," Jon Garland said. "Most managers played in the big leagues for some period of time, and as a player, sometimes you look at some of the decisions that are made or some of the things you hear, and you kind of look at him like, 'Hey, this game's not that easy. You should know that. You played it.' It seems like they're a little removed. Ozzie still seems like he's a little more in the game as a player. When he does things wrong, he thinks the same things a player would think about a manager. Like, 'What was I thinking right there? As a player, I wouldn't want to see that.' "

It's why he lets young players do their thing, bruises be damned. It's what he would have wanted as a player.

As for Viciedo, he would hit .255 with one home run and six runs batted in in twenty-nine games. He didn't turn out to be a savior, even a short-term one, in 2011.

·6·

FIND A MENTOR

John Kruk would like to formally apologize.

"I take 100 percent responsibility," he said, chuckling.

Few people in major-league baseball drop more F-bombs than Ozzie Guillen, and none do it with his dexterity. He might have learned the word during rookie ball in 1981, but he learned all of its combinations, tenses, applications, and nuances from Kruk, who was his teammate for three years in the minors, starting in Reno, Nevada, in 1982.

"He learned how to use it in a lot of different ways—a verb, an adverb, a noun, a pronoun," Kruk said. "It was free flowing. I apologize to people for that part of Ozzie's life. I feel like it is my fault."

So, yes, we have discovered the person who taught Guillen the many uses of the word *fuck*. It's like finding out who first put a paintbrush in Michelangelo's hand.

"He taught me all the wrong things," Guillen said, smiling.

Kruk doesn't really feel bad about being Ozzie's cursing coach, of course. Guillen without swear words would be like the rest of us without the word *the*. And it's not overstating things to say that part of his national reputation is built on four letters. He's the poet laureate of bleeps.

Kruk took Ozzie under his wing in Reno, and if you were going to be under Kruk's wing, you were going to swear. That was and is baseball.

"Teaching him that part of it might have been the most fun," said Kruk, who would go on to star as an outfielder and first baseman for the San Diego Padres and the Philadelphia Phillies and become a baseball analyst for ESPN. "I got him in trouble a couple times."

It wasn't without provocation, in Kruk's mind. Ozzie could be as insistent and irritating as a yapping puppy. He wanted to know everything—how to order a meal at a restaurant, how to pay the rent, why the manager made a certain move late in the game—everything. When Kruk would reach his breaking point, he'd purposely steer Guillen toward trouble, not that the young Venezuelan couldn't find it on his own.

"He'd piss me off," Kruk said. "A teammate would do something good in the game, and Ozzie would want to compliment him. He'd ask me, 'What do I say, Krukie?' I'd tell him to say something he shouldn't say, and the guy would get pissed and want to fight him.

"That was just my way of reining him in: 'Ozzie, you don't know everything yet. You're getting there, but it's going to take some time.' "

That's pretty much how Guillen remembers it, too, only with more terror and less breathing involved.

"One day, he told me to call a guy 'honey,' " he said. "I didn't know what it meant. Then another time, he told me to call another guy a name. The guy almost killed me. He was almost choking me. I'm not going to say what Kruk told me to say, but it was bad. Very bad."

Kruk was almost instantly taken with the loud and eager Guillen, who was three years his junior. Kruk had grown up in Keyser, West Virginia, population 5,200, and Guillen in Ocumare del Tuy, a city of about 140,000 people in northern Venezuela. Kruk went to junior college. Guillen didn't get past eighth grade.

But there were similarities: both were brash and noisy.

"I think Kruk and myself, we were kind of the same," Guillen said. "He wasn't a big prospect. Me either. And then all of a sudden, we were the best players on the team. It was a fat kid and a skinny kid playing. I think that's why we had feelings for each other. When I got married, he gave my wife a TV when we went on a road trip so she'd have something to do. We did a lot of things together."

Kruk saw something in the kid.

"A lot of Latin players when they come over here, they're intimidated by the language and the culture," he said. "Ozzie embraced it. He wanted to learn. He was eager to learn. He was asking questions—believe me—nonstop.

"I have two young children now. The 'Why, why, why' and the 'Why, Daddy?'—that was Ozzie to me. 'Why Krukie? Why this, Krukie? Why that, Krukie? What happened here, Krukie? Tell me this, Krukie.' I was like, 'Oh, God.' It's like what you do with your kids. You give them some candy, and maybe they'll be happy for a little while. But I didn't have any candy to give Ozzie."

Even though he was only playing Single-A ball in the Padres' minor-league system, Guillen was sure he was on his way up. He was certain he would be a big leaguer. Could *taste* it. In John Kruk, he saw someone on the same fast track who loved the game as much as he did. And he saw someone who was willing to lend a hand.

It helps to have a mentor in life, to have someone who will show you the ropes, the light, the way. That was Kruk for Ozzie.

Kruk gives Guillen a lot of credit for wanting to learn English, but really was there any choice? Depriving him of the ability to communicate clearly was a form of torture to him, even then. Imagine him not having the ability to talk about baseball, girls, politics, food, anything and everything. It's almost impossible, given the man we see, and hear, today.

"It was his personality," Kruk said. "He was very outgoing. I think he had a sense, 'I know I can play in the big leagues. If I do, and I want to be successful, I have to learn the language, and I have to be able to communicate with people.'

"Believe me, I'm not taking any credit for him being what he is today except for the language part. I played winter ball in Mexico, so I know what it's like to go to a foreign country and not be accepted—or having it take time to be accepted. I saw something in him, and I thought, 'You know what, we need to speed up the process with him.' So I tried to help him all I could.

"I helped him with language. I helped him with getting an apartment, helped him get his electric turned on. I let him know that you can't eat a hot dog every single day for every single meal. That was basically his language skills then. You try to help. I think besides the bad language, we've done a pretty good job, haven't we?"

Guillen admits his English was awful when he arrived

in Reno. That's why he became so reliant on Kruk. He said he was the only Latin player on the roster in a league with only a handful of Latin players. The Padres did not provide English lessons, as major-league organizations often do today.

"John helped me to get there quicker, to overcome quicker because I didn't have anybody to speak Spanish to," Guillen said. "Then I had to learn. Bad or good, I had to try to pick it up as soon as I could. It was hard, but I think John helped. When I was looking for an apartment, he made sure I lived close to him. When we went to a hotel, he made sure my room was close to his. When he went on the bus, he made sure I was behind or in front of him. We go to a restaurant, he made sure I sat next to him. All the little things I needed, he was there for me."

Guillen caused a stir in 2010 when he complained that major-league baseball offers privileges to Asian players that it doesn't extend to Latin players. He had been frustrated when he discovered that the White Sox' Single-A team his son Oney played on had a translator for a Korean player but none for the seventeen Latin players on the roster. It was a fairness issue, he said.

He'd prefer that Latin players embrace a new culture and language, which would eliminate the need for a discussion about translators. It's a message he'll bring to his new post in Miami. In Miami-Dade County, Hispanics make up 65 percent of the population, according to the 2010 U.S. Census, many of them having come to Miami from other countries for the same reasons Guillen came to the United States in 1981.

"I came here to make a lot of money," he said. "The only way I was going to make a lot of money was to learn the language. It's what I tell everybody here: You don't have to learn English, but it'll be easier for you if you do.

"If you want to have success in this country, you better get better with your English. There are people that have been here for thirty years, and they've always had an assistant next to them—do this, do that for me. In the meanwhile, they're wasting their time when they could be taking advantage of learning another language.

"They tell me they have a translator. I understand that. But in the meantime, try to help yourself to learn the language, just for the off-the-field stuff. It's more important."

Guillen knows the feeling of being trapped by a lack of language skills, of creating your own world in order to cope. He knows the feeling of not understanding what people around you are saying, of not wanting to be embarrassed, exposed. He knows the natural response to that is to not say anything.

It's not healthy. Guillen suspected as much when he came to the United States as a seventeen-year-old and knew it for sure a year later when John Kruk helped open a new world for him. And ever since, Guillen has tried to spread the importance of language skills to other Latinos. He does it with his players all the time.

Ozzie might have worn out his teammates with his incessant talking, but his mentor saw courage in it.

"How many Latin players could have been really good big-league players if they would have opened up and been more expressive?" Kruk said. "You see so many talented kids in the minor leagues who, because of the language barrier, just go into a shell. They don't live up to their potential because this is a scary place. Talent-wise, they're more than capable of being major-league players. The other things that are involved with that, Ozzie embraced it.

"He knew he didn't know the English language, but it didn't stop him from speaking it. He butchered the English language like you couldn't imagine. When you're speaking Spanish, the past tense, the present tense, that's the hardest part. You'll say the wrong word, and it sounds like you're talking about something completely different. It's kind of the same way with English. Ozzie would say stuff where you'd go, 'What's he talking about? Is he talking about yesterday or four days from now?'

"But he wasn't afraid. He knew he was going to mess up, that he was going to say the wrong thing but he was like, 'So what?' He said, 'They might not know what I'm saying, but they'll always know I'm talking.' "

There were obstacles along the way for Guillen. One day in 1984, when he was playing in Las Vegas, he wanted to take his wife out for dinner. They left their newborn, Ozzie Jr., with Kruk and Kruk's parents, who were visiting. The team had given each player a free-dinner coupon to one of the casino restaurants. First problem: the casino wouldn't allow the Guillens in because they were under twenty-one. Second problem: when they finally did find a way in and had enjoyed a nice meal, the restaurant informed them that the coupon had expired. Third problem: Ozzie had no money with him.

The restaurant manager allowed him to leave to get cash, but Ibis had to stay as collateral. Kruk's parents gave him money, and Guillen hustled back to give his wife her freedom.

That was life for Ozzie back then. He was learning something new almost every day, and it helped to have a more worldly friend alongside him—or as worldly as a twenty-three-year-old from West Virginia could be. Kruk was the one who got Guillen drunk for the first time.

Kruk had found his own mentor when he arrived in Reno two years earlier: Ozzie. Guillen was only eighteen at the time, but he knew more about baseball than any of the other players on the team. Part of it was that he had hung around with older players in Venezuela, but most of it had to do with the fact he absorbed information like a desert gulping rain.

"I came from a small town, and we didn't really know anything about positioning," Kruk said. "You could go to my high school field, and you'd see a spot in the grass in left where the left fielder had always stood. There was a spot in center, a spot in right, and a dip at short, third, second, and first where guys stood for every hitter.

"I played left field and I got to watch him. He moved around a lot. You could just tell he was studying hitters and our pitchers, how they would pitch people. He was just a smarter player than what we had. Even though I was three years older, I learned a lot about baseball just watching him."

People who spend time with Guillen know that he's easily distracted. It's not so much that he wants to be part of the action or even that he gets so wrapped up in the action he gets lost in it. It's that he likes to be nearby to comment on the action. His thoughts are like a nomadic tribe.

For three years, from Reno to Beaumont, Texas, to Las Vegas, a dust storm of chatter followed Kruk. Its name was Ozzie Guillen. If it had a title, it would be "Change of Subject."

"He'd sit there after an at-bat and say, 'What did you see? What did you see?'" Kruk said. "Then he'd say in the next second, 'What are we doing tonight? Where are we eating?' I was like, 'Let's try to finish this one off first before we decide where we're going. I'm not that smart, Ozzie. I got one thing on my mind right now, and that's this game.'

"He'd say, 'What about tomorrow? What are we doing tomorrow? You want to go to lunch tomorrow?' I was like, 'Ozzie, jeez.'"

If Guillen did tire out teammates with his constant jabbering, much of it was forgiven. People working together for the common good often grant space and accept eccentricities. Opponents? They're not so tolerant.

Guillen talked a lot on the field. A lot of Latin players did. Many came to the United States to play pro ball and were struck by the silence on the field. Where they came from, chatter was a way of keeping themselves mentally into a baseball game for nine innings. It's what Guillen did at shortstop.

There were also practical reasons for Guillen's gift of gab, even when he was growing up in Venezuela.

"When you play baseball and you're 130 pounds and you're fucking five-four, you better talk," he said. "People can't fucking see you, and they'll run you over. If you're six-three, three hundred, they will see you."

Guillen had been blessed with a lot of ability as a ballplayer, but power was not part of the blessings. So when he did hit a home run in the minors, he saw it as an opportunity to grab more attention. That didn't go over well on one occasion when he was playing Triple-A ball for the Las Vegas Stars.

"He did a little showboating around the bases like he could back then," Kruk said. "I was out in the outfield the next day shagging during batting practice, and their pitchers were running. I heard the pitcher who gave up the home run say, 'I'm going to pay whoever's pitching tonight a hundred dollars if they drill him.' It was another let's-take-care-of-Ozzie thing.

"I said, 'There's going to be some issues if he gets hit tonight. I want you to know that. So if you want to do it, do it. But I'm just telling you, if you do, you guys are going to have a lot more issues than what you care to have.' They didn't hit him."

Mentor, friend, bodyguard—Kruk was all of that to Guillen.

"I loved him, and I still do to this day," he said. "He was a joy. It was fun being a teammate of his. It was always entertaining. He would get upset if he had a bad at-bat. He used to break stuff all the time. Picture a seventeen-year-old kid playing professionally. He would break stuff. He'd get mad. He'd throw fits. Sometimes you had to talk him off the ledge, but we had a great relationship."

Ozzie was unpredictable. But you want true unpredictability? In 1995, Kruk signed with the White Sox as a designated hitter, but his heart wasn't in it, even if he was still having success at the plate. He singled against Baltimore in a game in late July, ensuring that his career average would be above .300, pulled himself from the game, and walked out of the park. He never played again.

He and Guillen were more alike than they'd probably care to admit. Both liked to talk. Both were driven to get to the majors. Kruk said it was worth any hearing loss he might have incurred dealing with the excitable one.

"It never got to be a burden," he said. "I played in the big leagues when young guys would come up, and you feel like it's a chore because you feel like you have to explain things to them over and over. He grasped. You'd say it one time and it was 'I got this.' The only thing he never did grasp was, 'Shut up, Ozzie.' Everything else, it was one time. You told him he couldn't do something, he wouldn't do it. You told him he couldn't say this, he wouldn't say it. You could tell at that age that he was going to be a guy who was going to be a good teammate and a really good player."

Kruk gladly kept an eye out for Ozzie.

"Always had to. And I wanted to," he said. "It wasn't like I had to. It was a very sad day when they traded him to the White Sox because I wish he would have been in San Diego with me when I got to the big leagues."

On December 6, 1984, the Padres traded the twenty-year-old Guillen, along with Tim Lollar, Bill Long, and Luis Salazar, to the White Sox for pitcher LaMarr Hoyt and two minor leaguers.

It meant two things. Ozzie was finally going to get his shot at the big leagues. And he was going to get heat because, only a year before, Hoyt had won the American League Cy Young Award. It didn't matter to some of Hoyt's teammates that his record had dropped from 24–10 in 1983 to 13–18 in 1984. What mattered was that they were losing a veteran pitcher who had helped lead the Sox to ninety-nine victories and a spot in the American League Championship Series in 1983.

"We traded a sure thing for three question marks," the White Sox' veteran catcher Carlton Fisk told the *Chicago Tribune* six weeks after the trade.

When Fisk talked, people took notes on stone tablets. The no-nonsense catcher was fourteen years into a twenty-four-year Hall of Fame career, and his comments carried weight. And here he was all but panning the trade.

"Guillen is supposed to be the next Luis Aparicio, right?" said Fisk, referring to the retired White Sox icon and Hall of Fame shortstop. "Well, we've seen a lot of those come and go, haven't we? It amazes me that people are passing off Hoyt as some nonentity traded for three other guys."

The comments reached Guillen in Venezuela. And just like that, what had been a time of joy went dark. If Carlton Fisk was against him, who would have the guts to be for him? Who would be his John Kruk this time?

There was a total eclipse of the sun on Planet Ozzie.

Manny Crespo, Guillen's rookie-ball mentor in Bradenton, Florida, had played with Fisk with the Red Sox' Double-A affiliate in 1970. Fisk called Crespo "Chico" and Crespo called Fisk "Pudge," like everybody else did.

"I get a call from Ozzie about one in the morning from Venezuela," Crespo said. "He said, 'Hey, Papa, did you hear about the trade?' I said, 'Yes, I'm happy for you. You're going to get a shot.' He said, 'Yeah, but you told me Carlton Fisk is your friend.' I said, 'Yeah, he's my friend.'

"Ozzie said, 'He said something in the paper, and it's going to be hard. He's the man in Chicago, and that could be very hard. I just want a legitimate shot. Can you call him and talk to him?' "

Two days later, Crespo was on the phone with Fisk. Crespo began by asking whether he had ever asked anything of Fisk. No, Fisk said, he couldn't think of one thing Crespo had ever asked for. What did he need? Money?

"You just traded LaMarr Hoyt for a young shortstop with the Padres," Crespo said.

"Yeah, can you believe that?" Fisk said. "I can't believe we made that kind of trade."

"Well, that's what I want to talk about. I need you to do me a favor. This kid is like my son."

There was a hard silence on the other end.

"Look, this guy's going to come to camp," Crespo continued. "I don't want you to help him, but I want you to just watch him. Give him a chance to see if he can make the club or not."

Fisk wanted to know about the young shortstop who had deprived the White Sox and their catcher of a standout pitcher.

"He's not the best defensive shortstop you've ever seen," Crespo said. "He doesn't have the best arm you've ever seen. He's not the fastest guy you've ever seen. He's not the best hitter you've ever seen."

"Stop right there, Chico," Fisk said, exasperated. "What *can* this guy do?"

"Pudge, this guy has got a huge heart, and all he wants to do is win. He's going to help you win games that you're going to be like, 'Oh, my God, how did he do that?' "

Fisk promised to watch and not say a word, to give the kid a chance without prejudging him on the basis of the very dumb decision the idiotic higher-ups in the Sox front office had made. It didn't mean he had to be happy about the trade. It meant he was going to give Ozzie a chance.

At the time, Crespo was working as a representative for the Worth baseball equipment company. During spring training, he traveled from team to team, making sure players who used Worth bats were happy with the product. He arrived at the White Sox site in Sarasota, Florida, about a week into spring training.

When Ozzie saw Crespo, he hugged him. Here was the first baseball man in the United States to truly believe in him.

All the hard work the two had put in together had paid off. It was a happy reunion.

Then a voice from the trainer's room cut through the euphoria.

"Chico!"

Crespo's stomach didn't exactly sink, but there was a definite tightening of the abdominal wall. He walked into the room where players were getting treatment.

"I need you to do *me* a favor now," Fisk said. "I need you to go over there and talk to your son and tell him to keep his mouth shut because he talks all the time and he still doesn't have one hit in the big leagues. Can you do that for me?"

"I can try, Pudge, but that's the guy's makeup," Crespo said.

"Oh, my Lord, Manny. He talks and talks the entire time."

"That's what keeps him sharp."

"I understand it if he's talking on the field, but he talks in the clubhouse like he's a Hall of Famer."

"Just watch him play," Crespo said.

Guillen made the club. He opened the season at shortstop and batted leadoff. Two weeks into the season, Crespo's phone rang at 2:00 a.m. Fisk wanted to know if he was calling too late. Other than the fact that it was 2:00 a.m. and he had been sound asleep, no, Pudge, it wasn't too late.

"Let me tell you about your son," Fisk said.

Here we go, Crespo thought. What had Ozzie done this time? Had he said the wrong thing? Had he said too much? Had he lost a game?

"It's a tie game, he's on second base, there's two outs," Fisk began. "There's a passed ball, and he takes off for third. The third-base coach is holding him. Your son rounds the base. He goes home, and he's safe, and we win the game by one run. I love watching this guy play."

Crespo was so relieved he could have cried in his pillow.

"But Manny, there's still one problem."

"What?" said Crespo, bracing himself.

"He's still talking."

Guillen didn't exactly find a mentor when he joined the White Sox in 1985. It was more like his mentors went and found him. He already had Luis Salazar, a fellow Venezuelan who was eight years his senior. Now he had Fisk, Harold Baines, Richard Dotson, Rudy Law, and the future Hall of Fame pitcher Tom Seaver, whose career was near its end. Tony La Russa was the manager. Jim Leyland was the third-base coach. A kid hungry to learn could have done a lot worse.

"I was lucky because those guys really took care of me, but they really taught me how to be a pro, how to play the game right, how to respect the game, how I go about my business," Guillen said. "I was lucky to learn when Tony was here, when Jim Leyland was here. If they saw something wrong on the field, they would come to you and tell you right away."

And then there was the ornery Seaver, who, at forty, was nineteen years older than the impetuous Ozzie.

"I was choked by fucking Tom Seaver once," Guillen said. "We were playing in New York and I hit a line drive. Dave Winfield dove for the ball and caught it. I slammed the fucking bat. When I came back, Seaver was waiting for me. He grabbed me by my shirt and pulled me all the way to the training room. He motherfucked me for a long time. He said, 'You're not that fucking good.' You learn from that. If older players did that shit now, everybody would say, [fake crying] 'Oh, God. Fuck.' That's why these rookies do whatever they fucking want to do because no player steps up in his ass. Now it has to be the manager or the coaches. I got my ass straightened out right away."

The player he most looked up to was Baines, who hardly ever talked. Not figuratively. Literally. Baines hardly talked. It was if Guillen had gone looking for his polar opposite on earth and found him. Maybe he was hoping some of Baines's calm and cool would rub off on him. But life doesn't work that way for Ozzie. A fire can stand next to a tree, but it will never turn into a tree.

Guillen was amazed at how self-controlled Baines was. He studied that impassiveness like a sociologist doing fieldwork.

"He could hit a home run with the bases loaded and strike out with the bases loaded, and it was the same," Ozzie said. "I don't think any player in the history of baseball carried himself the way Harold Baines did. He never got excited about anything. He never got upset by anything.

"It's not easy to play this game and be on the same level for that many years [twenty-two]. I think the only one who did it was Harold."

Guillen is quick to point out that he never found himself in a prolonged slump as a hitter and never seemed to have games when he struck out three or four times. That was probably a good thing for the sake of TVs and other possible targets of a certain shortstop's anger in the clubhouse.

"I was more pissed when I made errors than when I hit bad," he said. "Obviously, when I didn't hit, I was upset. But my game was defense. When I made an error, I was miserable. It's hard to beat Harold Baines at that. Good or bad, you'll throw a helmet or slam your bat or sit in a corner. I never saw him doing that."

Baines was the ideal he could never reach. It wasn't even

that Guillen aspired to be like him. He just enjoyed looking in wonder at the quiet one. How does a guy get 2,866 hits like that? It was beyond Guillen's comprehension how anybody could be so collected, but he admired it. Perhaps he couldn't be that way himself, but he could file it away for future reference. Sure enough, he ended up preaching it when he became a coach and a manager.

The decision to become a manager comes to people in different ways. Some aging players realize that they are married to the rhythms of a baseball season and can't live any other way. Some players want to be the ones who get to make the decisions. Some are born leaders.

And Ozzie? When did he have that epiphany? When did it dawn on him that he had something to offer to the game of baseball? When did he decide to become a manager?

"When I saw horseshit managers managing me," he said. "That's true. I was managed by a lot of horseshit managers. When people asked me, 'Do you think you'll be a manager?' I was like, 'Fuck, yeah! If this motherfucker is managing me, I should. I'm better than him, right now.' That's the truth. I played for some managers, it was like, 'How the fuck did you get that job?' "

For many White Sox fans, one of the low points in club history was the reign of Terry Bevington, who managed the team from 1995 to 1997. He was thirty-eight when he was hired, and the players were skeptical of his managerial skills. Those doubts seemed to be confirmed during a game in which he walked to the mound to remove a pitcher and had no one warming up in the bullpen.

But it was Bevington's lack of people skills that made Guillen fully understand that personality does matter for managers interested in motivating players. Bevington was the anti-mentor, the guy who taught Ozzie the valuable lesson of how not to be a manager.

It was Bevington who told Ozzie, in front of his teammates, to keep his young children out of the clubhouse, even though slugger Albert Belle was allowed to have his brother and his bodyguards regularly with him at his locker. If the world has learned anything about Guillen, it's that you don't mess with him when it comes to his family.

"Terry Bevington tried to pull some shit, and I told him to go fuck himself," he said. "That's the only manager I didn't respect in my career. Why? Because he was a piece of shit. If you don't respect your players, the players won't respect you. Then fuck you."

It wasn't as if there was a crowd of people who saw Guillen as a natural-born manager while he was playing. He was impulsive and a known human irritant. In 2001, the year after he retired, he took a job as the Montreal Expos' third-base coach when Jeff Torborg was brought in to replace Felipe Alou as manager. Guillen moved to the Florida Marlins the next year with Torborg, one of his former skippers in Chicago. Jack McKeon replaced Torborg thirty-eight games into the 2003 season, and Florida went on to win the World Series.

It was during his time with the Marlins that his friends saw a change in Guillen.

"I had thought he was coaching just because he was bored and he wanted something to do," Kruk said. "When the Marlins came to Philadelphia and played, I went down and talked to him. He had that passion, that same look he had in the minor leagues like, 'I'm getting to the big leagues and I'm going to be great and I'm going to be here a long time.' He had the same approach to managing. He was really inquisitive, asking questions to the other coaches and the manager. When I talked to the other coaches, they had that understanding, too, that this was a stepping-stone. It was not like, 'I want to be a third-base coach my whole life or a bench coach my whole life.' Not only did he want to be a manager, he wanted to be a great manager."

The story has been told and retold. When the Sox fired Jerry Manuel after the 2003 season, Kenny Williams went about the business of finding a replacement. Guillen, coming off a World Series with the Marlins, was on the interview list. The two had been teammates on the White Sox from 1986 to 1988, and Williams was familiar with Ozzie's loud ways. But Guillen had no managerial experience. Williams's first choice was Cito Gaston, who had won two World Series as the manager of the Toronto Blue Jays in the 1990s. After two interviews, it appeared to be Gaston's job.

But Williams still had to talk with Guillen, whom Jerry Reinsdorf had loved as a player. They brought him in the day after the Marlins had won the World Series. It looked like a courtesy interview. A favor. Or, at best, an interview with an eye toward the future, when perhaps Guillen would be more seasoned.

It didn't turn out to be the gesture Williams had thought it would be. The interview started at noon and didn't end until 4:15 p.m.

"I'm going to be me," Guillen told Williams to start the interview. "If you like it, you hire me. If you don't, make sure you pay for another first-class ticket to get me back home."

Williams was concerned that Guillen's "goofball side" would lead to players, fans, and the media not taking him seriously. A hurricane named Ozzie quickly swept away that concern.

"By two p.m., I decided Ozzie was going to be the next manager," Williams said. "The passion, the commitment, the energy, the game knowledge, the aggressive attitude, and I liked that he looked me in the eye."

If Williams had looked closely at Guillen's eyes, he might have noticed how hungover he was from an epic night of partying that took place after Florida had won the championship. The three-hour flight to Chicago wore off the buzz, but it couldn't do anything about the headache.

A few days later, Guillen flew back to Chicago for a second interview. This one came right after the Marlins' victory parade in Miami. Same thing: Ozzie was hungover. This time, Reinsdorf and Williams offered him the job. His only explanation for his condition not getting in the way is that Reinsdorf and Williams probably believed he was tired from the excitement of winning a World Series.

Whatever he was—shaky and hungover or as sober as a judge—he was now the manager of the Chicago White Sox. All the managers Guillen had played for or coached with played one role or another in getting him there, but most notably Tony La Russa, Jim Fregosi, Jeff Torborg, Gene Lamont, Bobby Cox, and Jack McKeon. And, yes, even Terry Bevington, who Guillen thought had a decent grasp of the game, despite their differences.

Kruk sees the accumulation of all that knowledge and experience in the way Guillen runs a team. He doesn't burn out pitchers. He doesn't abuse his bullpen. He tries to give his relievers rest. He tries to keep the atmosphere light and fun.

And there's even a little bit of Harold Baines to him.

"The great thing about Ozzie is that I think he understands that it's 162 games. Some people get lost in that," Kruk said. "They think, 'This is the most important game we're going to play.' They don't understand that we have four or five months left in the season. That's the way he approached the game. He still had a temper when he was playing with the White Sox, but I think he understood, 'Okay, I was 0-for tonight, but tomorrow, I'm going to get three hits.' I think he takes that into his managing."

There's some Tom Seaver mixed in, too. In 2004, his first season as manager, Guillen was furious with outfielder Carlos Lee for not sliding hard into second base to break up a double play and get some payback against Minnesota. The Twins' Torii Hunter earlier had plowed over Sox catcher Jamie Burke, knocking him out of the game. It's why the Sox traded Lee to Milwaukee after the season. *Play the game right. Respect the game. Defend your teammates. Send a message, if necessary.*

All those influences aside, whatever Ozzie is now personality-wise comes from his inherent Ozzieness. None of the people he played with and for could mold that. There's only one Say Anything Kid.

And there's only one manager who would react the way Guillen did to a small brush fire in early August of the 2011 season.

Alex Rios had jogged, rather than sprinted, after a ball that was hit over his head in a game against the New York Yankees at the Cell. His lack of hustle was a topic of conversation on the radio talk shows the next day. The consensus seemed to be that Guillen should have benched Rios again, on the spot. Not playing hard—wasn't that the biggest no-no in Ozzie's book?

This being Guillen, the conversation veered in a direction no one had expected.

"Let me explain to the idiots out there, the geniuses," he told reporters. "They say I don't bench Rios, but the only player I bench [earlier in the season] because he didn't hustle, it was Rios, for two days, okay? . . . Tell these people out there, they think they know baseball more than me, then send me the lineup that was better without Rios in the lineup. Is Rios not playing well? Of course he's not, he's brutal everywhere. People think I don't know. Yes, I know. People think Rios doesn't know. Of course he knows. That's common sense.

"If you think . . . I'm playing him because he's Latino, [I'm not]. You know how many Latino players I get rid of here? Every time the people talk about it, it's a bunch of crap. I want to know how many managers take the players out of the game, during the game, now. You see any manager call the guy in, especially when he makes $56 million for the next three years, [and tell him] 'Get your ass out of there because you're not playing the way we should be playing'? Me!"

So here was Guillen going on a rant and then defending himself against accusations that he favors Latin players, even though no one was sure who had accused him of it. A Sox fan who had written something on a message board or in a tweet? Who knew? It only takes a spark to start a fire, but in this case, no one knew what the spark was. The one certainty was that Ozzie was holding the bellows.

At the time, there were people in Chicago who had grown tired of Guillen and his outbursts. A weariness had set in among some fans. You talk as much as he talks, and it can get old faster than Nick Nolte.

But what was the alternative? No Ozzie? Be careful what you wish for.

"Are some of his rants hilarious? Yes," Kruk said. "You don't think the players get a kick out of listening to him sometimes? If I was a player, after a game I'd want to hear what he was saying just to hear what he was saying."

But sometimes it's not so funny. In 2006, Guillen called *Chicago Sun-Times* columnist Jay Mariotti a "fucking fag" after Mariotti had written a critical column about him. Guillen was frustrated that Mariotti never showed up in the Sox clubhouse after ripping the manager or the team. He saw this as a complete lack of courage. Commissioner Bud Selig ordered Guillen to undergo sensitivity training.

Of the two two-hour sessions with the counselor, Guillen told reporters, "I think the guy learned more from me than I learned from him."

In 2005, the White Sox signed Tadahito Iguchi, who had starred in Japan, to play second base. A small but steady stream of Japanese players had been coming to the United States since Hideo Nomo first tasted success for the Los Angeles Dodgers in 1995.

Several Japanese newspapers already were staffing Sox games because reliever Shingo Takatsu was in his second year with the team, but the arrival of Iguchi raised their interest level. The Japanese writers assigned to the team already had a season's worth of Ozzie under their belt. Something had been bothering them.

"One of the female writers came up to me and said, 'Some of the reporters have asked me to ask you what some of the words that Ozzie uses mean,'" said Joe Goddard of the *Sun-Times*. "I'm thinking to myself, 'How am I going to explain *motherfucker* and how am I going to explain *asshole*?'

"But I tried. I said, 'MF means that you would make love to your own mother.' She stared at me with her eyes big. I said, 'Asshole means where you have a bowel movement from.' Now she's really stunned.

"Finally, she says, 'Our men don't talk that way.' I said, 'Don't take it literally. It's just how he talks.' "

·7·

DON'T CONFUSE TEAM AND FAMILY

If Ozzie Guillen's office at the Miami Marlins' new ballpark is like the one he had in Chicago, it will be a photographic ode to his family. There will be pictures everywhere on the walls. There will be a studio portrait of Ozzie, Ibis, and their three sons: Ozzie Jr., Oney, and Ozney. There will be a photo of Ozzie and his family in front of a Christmas tree. There will be a photo of the family with President George W. Bush. There will be more than fifty photos of the Guillens in various stages of stick-togetherness.

"People don't know this: we eat together at home every day," Ozzie Jr. says. "We barely miss lunchtime together. You see him, you'll see at least one of the three of us [sons]. In that aspect, we're very close. My dad doesn't surround himself with big entourages. He always has us around."

For his players, there are more than a few positives that flow out of Ozzie's intense feelings about family. Many managers talk a good game about giving players time off to deal with personal matters, but there's implicit pressure to keep the distractions to a minimum.

Not so with Guillen.

"If you have anything with your family, as soon as the words start to come out of your mouth, he tells you to do what you have to do," Paul Konerko said. "He's not hard in that way. He's very soft in that way. I think people see him as a hard figure, and he is on some things, but I think when it comes to family, he's not.

"That would probably be the one thing that would surprise people. When it comes to your kids, your wife, your mom, your dad, any relation, or a friend, he doesn't mind that getting in the way of us winning tonight. He's been that way since day one. I've never seen him miss on that, as far as doing it sometimes and not other times.

"When someone has a problem or an issue, if it has to do with your family, it always takes precedence over this."

Managers and coaches forever are trying to create a "family" atmosphere with their team, in the hopes that any extra closeness it might bring about will somehow translate into more victories. How many times have you heard a player or a coach describe his team as a family? If spending most of your time with thirty players and coaches qualifies as a family, then perhaps a baseball team is a family. But most parents don't put their children on waivers, as tempting as that might be at times. There had been moments when the idea of the Guillens waiving the blunt Oney would have gained strong support among baseball fans in Chicago.

Ozzie knows where his loyalty lies, and of this there is no gray area. There is one family, the Guillens. And his biggest issues as manager of the White Sox, those that eventually helped push him out the door, had to do with his family. If the Marlins are smart, they will go out of their way to make all five members of the family feel part of the organization. Woe to them if they don't.

American business is full of father-and-son shops. Family ties are not roadblocks to success. But the family dynamic with the Guillens is . . . *involved*. You have Ozzie, who is a cauldron of words and emotions, and you have Oney, who is Mini-Me to Ozzie's Dr. Evil. Of the three sons, he is most like the father. Same outspokenness. Lots of the same opinions. Same primal need to tweet.

In May 2011, Chet Coppock, a longtime sports radio personality in Chicago who himself is no stranger to bombast, tweeted, "Hey, Ozzie, when are you going to bench Dunn and his $56 million contract?"

Oney didn't wait long to tweet back, "When ur mom cums on my face for once."

What do you do when your son lashes out like that publicly? If you're Ozzie Guillen, you don't do anything. Few people in Chicago noticed the tweet, so it was a variation of the philosophical question of a tree falling in a forest when no one is around.

This one didn't make much of a sound, but it pointed to the bigger issue of whether mixing family and work is a good thing for a manager and the more specific issue of why Ozzie refuses to do anything to rein in his son.

And if he can't rein in his son, how will he be able to rein in his players, when it becomes necessary?

Guillen refers to the 2010 season as "hell." It began when Kenny Williams called Oney, who was working in the team's video-scouting department, into his office before spring training. If there had been some ominous, foreboding music available, it would have been a good time to play it.

Oney had tweeted that the White Sox should re-sign their catcher A. J. Pierzynski. It didn't look good that the manager's son, an employee of the organization, was openly campaigning for the team to shell out money to a particular player. His nose was where it didn't belong. Perhaps Williams didn't want Pierzynski back with the team. Or maybe Jerry Reinsdorf didn't. Who knew? It didn't matter that Oney Guillen was about one rung from the ground on the Sox' organizational ladder. All anyone who followed Oney on Twitter could see was that he wanted Pierzynski back. One would be forgiven for inferring that his words carried some weight, seeing as how he was the manager's son.

Williams asked him to stop tweeting about the team.

What followed was the type of firestorm that only can happen with Ozzie and the Family Guillen. The Guillens already were frustrated at what they saw as the Sox' resistance to Ozzie starting his own website. In subsequent tweets, Oney criticized the food and service at Market, a Chicago restaurant. It "hands down" had the "worst food in the city," he tweeted. Oney as restaurant critic would have been fine if it weren't for the fact that Kenny Williams co-owned Market.

Now the conflict was out in the open.

It was Ozzie who made Oney resign from his position with the team, but ownership and the front office were tired of his Twitter act. However, it was clear from Ozzie's rare media boycott on the day of Oney's departure that he was stewing about the treatment of his son.

There were deeper issues involved. Ozzie had said many times that he considered Reinsdorf a father figure. It wasn't a stretch to see Guillen and Williams competing for Reinsdorf's approval. In this instance, Williams had won. Whenever

Williams referred to the Oney tweets, he called them "peripheral things" that took away from the business at hand, which was baseball. But in Guillen's mind, family can never be peripheral.

He knew that Oney shouldn't have been tweeting about White Sox personnel issues. It didn't mean he had to be serene about what he viewed as Williams's attempts to control everything.

"The side story is I actually tried to save Oney," Williams said, recalling a meeting he had with Ozzie and Reinsdorf after Oney resigned. "We had had enough. We really didn't like some of the things that were going on, but I've raised my own boys. It takes a while sometimes to grow up.

"Ozzie and I were alone in his office after Jerry left. I said, 'You know, I think we need to sleep on this. Let's have a conversation with him. Let's give him a chance.' He said, 'No, I've had enough. This is bullshit.'

"I'm a little more forgiving, probably too forgiving in some ways. That was one I was willing to cut some slack on. People have said so much shit about me over eleven years, you become immune to it. You think I'm really going to worry about that? I would rather Oney not do it because there are obvious problems associated with it. But anything personal toward me, I don't really give a shit."

It was the beginning of the end for Guillen with the White Sox, even if no one saw it that way at the time. The manager believed a line had been crossed. Not by Oney but by the team. They had fooled with his family. There was no relieving him of this notion.

On his way out, Oney tweeted: "I hope the dorks aren't running the organization or else we're fucked. 3 geeks who never played baseball a day in there [*sic*] life," referring to some of the people in the front office.

And Ozzie added his own tweet: "Hey kid we are behind you. No matter what."

Later, Ozzie tweeted in Spanish, "They touched me where it hurt most and I have to be ready for whatever comes."

The characteristics that make Guillen deal so effectively with players are the same characteristics that caused his problems in Chicago. There is no such thing as partial loyalty to him. He's loyal to the hilt, as he would show with Adam Dunn, Juan Pierre, and Gordon Beckham throughout the 2011 season. So if the Sox thought the Oney situation was over, that it would calm down like a pot taken off a stove, they were sorely mistaken. Ozzie would never forget.

What seemed obvious to most people—that you can't have the son of the manager talking about the team in public—wasn't so obvious to Guillen. To this day, he defends Oney's right to criticize the team, as long as he's not working for the organization.

"He's an adult," Guillen said.

Williams saw it the other way: "If it was my kid, my size twelve would be straight up his ass. There would be no further problem. But that's why they call it 'your' family. You have a right to raise and love your family however you want. I've got other shit to worry about."

But, really, did anyone believe Ozzie would raise his children to be diplomats?

"We come from a family that says that you have to say what's on your mind on what you believe," Ozzie Jr. said. "When it comes to Oney, I think it would be hard for my dad to say, 'You can't say this.' Because then Oney could say, 'Well, you can't say this then.' You'd be a hypocrite."

After the 2010 season, Oney Guillen would go on to rip Bobby Jenks, who had criticized Ozzie after signing with the Red Sox. Lesson: If you take on one Guillen, you take on them all.

For some of the players, the problem was that Oney Guillen acted as if he were a player on the team. They were quick to point out that very fact after he had tweeted about Jenks's alleged drinking and marital problems. Reliever Matt Thornton, in particular, was unhappy that a player's issues hadn't stayed in the clubhouse, a sacred place to the people who had lockers there.

It raised a bigger issue that might have affected Ozzie's ability to counsel his players. Is it safe to tell the manager your personal problems? Or is he going to tell his son, the serial tweeter?

"I don't know how it's going to affect guys who have that kind of relationship with Ozzie where they have to disclose personal information with him and talk about personal things," Thornton said in a radio interview at the time. "It might. You never know. . . . You can't have those kind of worries."

Guillen said that Oney's information about Jenks's problems had come from other people in the organization, not from him.

If you're looking for the accelerant that helped turn the simmering conflict between Guillen and Williams into a raging fire, it was the Major League Baseball draft.

As the annual selection day approached in June 2010, the Guillens had high hopes for Ozney, the youngest of the three boys and a talented high school outfielder. They thought he might be taken as high as the tenth round, which would bring a decent signing bonus. The White Sox chose him in the twenty-second round, where the money is thin.

Making matters much, much worse was the fact that the Sox had taken Williams's son, Kenny Jr., in the sixth round of the 2008 draft. The sports team as family? It looked to Guillen as if some family members were getting preferential treatment over others. And he fumed.

It led to an intervention by Reinsdorf.

"I said, 'You guys can't have this kind of bullshit. You have to work together,'" the team chairman told reporters. "That was basically it. Go make up. I didn't use those words. I said we can't function if you are not going to get along. You can have your fights like you always have, but it can't continue because we can't function that way. They both agreed and as far as I know, they are back to normal."

Major-league baseball has a history of teams drafting sons of members of their organizations. It's not exactly one of the spoils of winning the war to get to the top of the management food chain, but it happens. The Sox had chosen Oney Guillen in the thirty-sixth round of the 2007 draft. He played two years in their minor-league system, hitting .215.

In 2005, the Seattle Mariners drafted pitcher Worth Lumry, whose 1–2 record and 8.41 earned-run average for Princeton University weren't as impressive as the fact that he was a son of a member of the Mariners' ownership group. Hell, former White Sox general manager Ron Schueler chose his *daughter* in the forty-third round of the 1993 draft.

But none of that mattered to the Guillens now. What mattered was that the Sox brass had allowed Ozney, groomed to be a ballplayer from the time he could walk, to publicly free-fall to the twenty-second round out of high school. Never mind that all the other teams had passed on him in the preceding rounds as well. To Ozzie, it was personal.

It would get more personal in 2011, when Ozney, then playing for a community college in Miami, didn't get drafted at all. It was the stuff of winces.

On the day Ozney was passed over, Ozzie fired off a series of tweets that seemed full of anger.

"No matter how hard it is, yes, keep going and fighting to the end."

"The best of my life is not here yet, is coming, I am a warrior with a lot of heart and marbles."

"What can I ask? Nothing. Keep going to make this better to the people who love me."

"I grow up with nothing. I work all my life. Great family and good friends. Health and a lot of love."

"To the people who care and love me."

"God grab your neck but never choke."

The tweets were the subject of much discussion on the radio talk shows, with people trying to decipher their meaning. The consensus was that he was furious his son hadn't gotten drafted, and the stormy look on Guillen's face that day seemed to back it up. He would later say he was upset about a sick friend in Venezuela.

Who knew with Ozzie?

With their first pick in the 2011 draft, the White Sox had taken Central Arizona's Keenyn Walker, a center fielder who had also starred in football in high school. This led to a tweet from—surprise!—Oney Guillen: "Shocker white sox pick another black kid good athlete. How about picking a good baseball player?"

The opinion was Oney's, but part of it was right out of his dad's book. It fell perfectly in line with Ozzie's contention that a dual-sport athlete is a house divided. He likes players who have devoted their lives to baseball, as he did. The constant repetition. The tedium of taking grounder after grounder. The grunt work that builds ballplayers.

And, hmmm, who else was black and had been a two-star athlete? Why, Kenny Williams himself! He had been a football and baseball player at Stanford before the White Sox drafted him in the third round of the 1982 draft.

There's a possible explanation for why Guillen refused to demand that Oney stop tweeting about the Sox. He agreed with Oney's opinions. It was a way of getting his point across without actually moving his own lips or, this being Twitter, his fingers.

The Guillens were also upset with how the White Sox had handled Ozney in the lead-up to the draft.

"It wasn't about Ozney not getting drafted," Ozzie Jr. said. "There were thirty teams that didn't draft him. But [the White Sox] made him come out here and try out for the scouts, tell him everything's fine, making this big show, and the draft comes around and nothing.

"I don't think Oney's tweet helped the second day [of the draft]. But was everyone thinking what he had tweeted? Yes, everybody thought the same thing, but nobody wrote about it.

"Kenny's the general manager. If I was in his position, I might have done the same. It's his team. I didn't want Ozney to get picked as a favor to my dad. If they didn't believe he's good enough, then don't pick him. Go to school one year and play wherever you've got to play. Sometimes, you've got to step outside and look at this as a business."

The Sox already had been through enough drama with Oney, and that had gone into their decision not to draft Ozney in 2011. How long would it be before Ozzie thought the Sox should promote Ozney from Single-A to Double-A? Or from Double-A to the majors? And how long before Oney tweeted his displeasure with how the Sox were dealing with his brother? It would be an issue that would never go away.

"Let's just say that we felt there was potential for even more distractions," Williams said.

When you hire Ozzie Guillen to be your manager, you're hiring his family, too. There is no separation of church and state. It's all entwined. The man calling the shots from the dugout is the same man who told the *Chicago Sun-Times* in February 2011 that he'd kill anyone who messes with his sons.

"I don't think I have the best kids in the world, but I don't have the worst," he said. "I think that's why life's all fucked up. Some parents don't give a fuck what their kids do. They don't protect them. They don't talk to them.

"Family's the only thing you have. I didn't have the family I wanted to have growing up. If you don't have a good family, your family is not going to be the family you want. The most painful shit you can have is to have kids. That's the worst thing ever is to have kids. They make you smile for two minutes, and then they make you crazy for twenty-four hours. That's not just my kids. It's everybody's kids.

"If you don't care, then fuck it. When you care and you worry, it's hard. You want their life to be better. You wish they didn't do stuff or say stuff, but you can't control that. That's why I protect my family."

Guillen's fierce devotion to his family and to his team comes from being the child of a broken home. It informs everything he does, good and bad.

Guillen was born in Ocumare del Tuy, Venezuela, on January 20, 1964. When he was nine years old, his parents split up. He talked them into putting him in a boarding school in the nearby town of Los Teques because, he said, he didn't want to have to choose between them. By eighth grade, he had decided he was done with school. For all intents and purposes, he was on his own.

He said he never got over his parents' divorce. When he was a child, the only thing that helped fill the hole in his life was sports. He played basketball. And he was good enough at volleyball to be on a Venezuelan national youth team, though no one would call Venezuela the Fertile Crescent of volleyball. His least favorite sport was the one that would provide a very good living for him.

"The last profession I wanted was to play baseball," he said. "I didn't like it. It was boring to me. I was playing more basketball and volleyball because it was more fun. When we picked a team to play volleyball, we needed twelve guys. To play baseball, we needed like twenty guys, and nobody wanted to do it."

One day, when he was about eleven years old, Guillen and a number of other boys were taking grounders. A ball took a nasty hop and hit him in the mouth, opening a cut. A few moments later, Ernesto Aparicio, the uncle of the Hall of Fame shortstop Luis Aparicio, was standing over him.

"Look where the ball hit you," he said. "It means you didn't take your eye off the ball. You're going to be a shortstop."

And from then on, he was.

Guillen's father had played for town teams—the Venezuelan equivalent of Single-A ball—and he wanted more for his son. The two sports Ozzie was playing that involved nets weren't going to get him anywhere. The one with bats was a different story.

His father had a question for him.

"What are you going to feed a family with? Medals?" he said. "You had better go play baseball. This is the best chance you have to become something."

He took the advice to heart. Too much to heart. He stopped going to school at thirteen to focus on baseball in Guarenas, a city east of Caracas, the capital.

"My dad never saw me play until my first game in professional baseball," he said. "He had said, 'You've got to go to school.' I said, 'I don't want to go to school.' Then it was, 'Okay, get the fuck out of my life.'

"Now there are more Venezuelan players because of the bad economy. Everybody looks at Miguel Cabrera and says to their kids, 'Look at what he's making. You're a baseball player, fuck school.' When I was growing up, your parents wanted you to be a doctor because baseball was shit. Nobody cared about baseball then."

Guillen was a natural at the game. The footwork and the throwing ability were already there. And he wasn't afraid of sweat. The bigger question was whether he could stay on the straight and narrow in the horrible conditions in and around Caracas. Drugs and prostitution were everywhere.

"I raised myself," he said. "I could have gone either way. I could have gone and sold drugs and killed people and lived in the street. Or I could raise a family with a nice woman, try to get my life the way it is and not make an excuse for anything. I took it as an opportunity to raise myself the way I wanted to be raised.

"I never thought I was going to make this much money

and be manager of a big-league club, but I worked for it. If I was somebody else, I might have said, 'Fuck, I'll stay in Guarenas and hang around with my friends, be on the corner.' I never did drugs, thank God. But I was fucking fourteen, and maybe right now I'd be selling shit to survive.

"You had two opportunities. You can take the right one or the wrong one. Everybody in life does that. You go the wrong fucking way, you'll be a loser the rest of your life. A lot of people say, 'Oh, I'm not lucky. The government doesn't do this.' Fuck. My wife and I, we were carrying buckets of water to take a shower. When we took a shit, we had to go all the way down to get water to put in the toilet. That's the way we grew up."

In 2011, when the actor Sean Penn stated that Venezuelan president Hugo Chavez was not a dictator, Guillen tweeted, "Sean Penn if you love Venezuela, please move to Venezuela for a year . . . but please move to Guarenas or Guatire to see how long you last clown."

Guillen used to take his wife and kids back to Guarenas often, but over the years it became more dangerous, and the trips became less frequent. A crack cocaine epidemic turned the area into a war zone in the 1990s.

"I've been back there," said Ozzie Jr. "It's Vietnam all over again. You can talk about any bad neighborhood in the United States, and I'd be fine being in one of those neighborhoods than being from where he's from. In Venezuela, they're averaging sixty murders a weekend.

"Where he's from in Venezuela, it's a very easy place to go down the wrong path. It's not even considered different. It's just what people do. It's surprising for him to be as focused coming from a broken home, basically being on his own, for him not to go down that road. He's got a lot of friends in jail. A lot of friends have passed away. Now it's worse than it used to be. Now it's ten times worse. But it would have been really, really easy for him to say, 'I can do whatever I want, not be married, not have a family, and do all the bad things.' To come from where he's come from and succeed is very special."

Ozzie met Ibis at a bus stop in Guarenas when he was sixteen years old. He invited her to skip the line and stand with him. He began telling people she was his girlfriend, despite the fact that he had not actually informed her of this development. Not long after, he signed a contract with the San Diego Padres and left for rookie ball in Florida with wide eyes and big dreams. Three years later, he married Ibis.

Guillen says if he had been in his parents' shoes, he never would have allowed his child to move to the United States at seventeen. But baseball was a way out. And to this day, it makes him appreciate what he has.

"The biggest mistake parents do is to say, 'I want my kids to have better stuff than I have. I want my kids to live better than we did,'" Guillen said. "Fuck you. You're going to live the way we live. I didn't have a car. My kid shouldn't have a car when he's sixteen. No. It's the wrong way. I'm going to raise my kid the way I think he should be raised, not because of the way I was raised. That's a big mistake. The only good thing about it is, I tell my kids, is they get better vacations. That's it. I wish my kids were fucking raised the way I was raised. They might have better common sense about life and appreciate things."

He wouldn't allow his boys to drive until they were eighteen. However, it does help to have friends with truckloads of disposable income. Oney's first car was a used Lexus, given to him by the former major leaguer Ugueth Urbina, who said he felt bad when he noticed the boy's friends all had nice rides. Ozzie sighed and gave in.

Guillen's upbringing in an achingly poor area helped him in dealing with all sorts of people. He said he feels comfortable conversing with anyone, no matter the person's pedigree or bank account. It has helped him as a manager. He can discuss anything with anybody, from stars to utility players.

"I can talk to you. I can talk to Chavez. I can talk to Obama. I can talk to a fucking guy on the street," he said. "I'm not better than anybody out there. That's why I made one comment years ago: You put me with Bill Gates, I might not know anything about technology, but I can talk to his people. But if I told Bill Gates to go to my hometown, we'll see how long he'll fucking last. He'd say, 'What the fuck do I say here? What should I do here?' Because he never went through it. I went through it all my life."

Guillen says when he returns to Venezuela, he finds himself hanging out with poor people more often than not.

"People are like, 'Why are you drinking with them?'" he said. "That's me. That's the way I am. I don't care. I never lived the high life. People say, 'Well, you've got a nice house.' Fuck, yeah, I earned it. I have a boat. I earned it. I don't hang around with the high-life people. I could go everywhere with the big people. I don't. I hang out with the same fucking people in Venezuela. I go to the bullfight with my wife and a couple friends, that's it. After the bullfight, I go home. I'm not as social as people think.

"I grew up, don't make an excuse or point somebody else out. I always take full responsibility for my actions. It's kind of weird. I have the same friends all my life. We eat in the same restaurants. If you see me in Venezuela, I have no shoes on, shorts, driving a fucking motorcycle, saying hi to everyone. That's the way I am. I don't have a fucking chauffeur. I don't have a bodyguard. I've got the same guy working for me for the last thirty years.

"I can show you a picture from Christmas 1980 and I can show you a picture from Christmas 2010. Same fucking people, just bigger, older, with kids. I don't have friends richer than me. They're normal workers. I know a lot of people with great jobs, but they're not my friends. I can sit down and talk with Chavez in the same way I can sit down with somebody with no clothes on."

Guillen still goes back to Venezuela every year. It's not always pleasant. He sees some people who have given up, who have taken the easy way out. It angers him.

"People say, 'You don't help anybody,'" he said. "I don't *need* to help anybody. I do it just because I *want* to help other people. I put my time in a lot of hospitals in Venezuela not because I want to be noticed but because I know some people don't have anything. I want to help.

"A lot of people in my hometown say, 'You don't like me anymore?' Fuck you, losers. They say, 'Oh, you think you're richer.' Yes, motherfucker, I am. Fuck, yeah. I'm a Venezuelan icon. Fuck you guys. You made your choice. It's easy to live this way. It's hard to live my way.

"It's easy to live like, 'Who gives a fuck? I only have one pair of pants.' It's harder when you have an education and you have to pay for your kids. That's a hard life. When you don't care about life, then you live that way. They don't have anything to hope [for]."

Does Guillen's upbringing help his managing? It certainly

has given him the ability to understand players who come from impoverished backgrounds. And he is keenly aware of the obstacles Latin players have to overcome to make it to the big leagues. He caused that stir in 2010 when he said Asian players are treated better in baseball than Hispanic players. Asian players are assigned translators, he said, while Latin players often aren't. But that has to do with the relatively few Asians in baseball and the isolation they face. In 2010, 27 percent of major-league players were Hispanic and 2.3 percent were Asian, according to a University of Central Florida study.

Guillen is very protective of Hispanic players but also very demanding. He doesn't necessarily hold them to a higher standard than non-Latinos, but he believes he knows where they come from, geographically and culturally. Thus, there's no fooling him.

In 2005, after the outfielder Magglio Ordonez left the White Sox to sign a five-year, $75 million contract with the Detroit Tigers, he accused Guillen of negatively influencing his contract negotiations with the White Sox. It set off Guillen like few things have. Ordonez was a fellow Venezuelan, so he was family on multiple levels.

There was rage, hurt, and betrayal in Ozzie's response. Mostly rage.

"He's a piece of shit," Guillen said at the time. "He's another Venezuelan motherfucker. Fuck him. He thinks he's got an enemy? No, he's got a big one. He knows I can fuck him over in a lot of different ways. He better shut the fuck up and just play for the Detroit Tigers."

That incident led to a broader question. Do all of his blowups, big and small, affect his ability to deal with his players?

"Who can play for a guy who would ridicule you in front

of the media and fans?" SI.com's John Donovan wrote of Guillen's tongue-lashing of Ordonez. "What highly paid gazillionaire modern athlete can do his best when he's worried about what his manager might be saying behind his back? This is what got Larry Bowa into deep bleep in Philadelphia. This is what eats away at a manager's credibility, no matter how good an on-field wizard he might be."

The answer to Donovan's original question is easy. Players who want to win a World Series want to play for Ozzie. The Sox ended up winning the title that season, without Ordonez. And it's why the Marlins wanted Guillen so badly in 2010 and 2011. Players want to play for him, and they want to play hard for him.

But he's not for everyone, not even close. In 2006, Dodgers coach Mariano Duncan, a Dominican Republic native, said that Guillen's outspokenness was hurting other Latinos' chances of becoming managers.

"He embarrassed every Latino player, coach, and front-office person," Duncan told the *Los Angeles Times*. "Ozzie is a hero in his country and a hero in my country. We are here in America, where you can speak freely. But you don't say everything that comes to your mind. He has to learn to slow down a little bit. You have to learn how to close your mouth."

Ozzie, close his mouth? What's he supposed to do, hum his opinions?

"Mariano Duncan never will be a big-league manager and not because I ruined it for him," Guillen said. "If Mariano Duncan thinks being a manager is making out the lineup and changing pitchers, he is real wrong."

In 2011, Duncan was the hitting coach for the Tennessee Smokies, the Chicago Cubs' Double-A affiliate.

• • •

Ozzie Guillen says he's shy.

No, really.

"I talk at the ballpark, but in my house I'm pretty quiet," he said. "I'm shyer than people think I am."

Shy? The guy who could talk the ears off an elephant? The man given to exaggeration? The man who made a big show of telling Graham Bensinger of Yahoo! Sports that he was drunk both times he interviewed for the White Sox managerial job in 2003, only to clarify weeks later that he was, in fact, merely hungover?

That guy is shy?

"I walk to the restaurant, and I feel weird," Guillen said. "I go to the same place most of the time because I don't like to be bothered. Believe me, if I know you, it's a different thing. But if I walk somewhere, people think I'm high-fiving everybody. I'm very shy about that. Very. When I walk the dog in the streets and people say hi, I say, 'What's up?' I never put my head up. I keep walking. I'm shyer than people think I am. Very. Very. But after the first pitch, I'm going to talk to somebody. People would be surprised if they could see me off the field. It's a different life."

Kenny Williams didn't buy it.

"He must not know what 'shy' means in English," the White Sox general manager said.

The shy guy enjoys barbecuing on his deck at home. He enjoys cooking, period. He likes watching cable news programs. He's interested in all things Spain. He reads books and appreciates art.

The shy guy is a bleeping Renaissance man?

"It will be interesting the day he stops being a manager,"

Ozzie Jr. said. "What's he going to do? Is he going to leave the game and go to Spain forever and be on his boat? I couldn't see my dad being a broadcaster on an everyday basis. He wouldn't want to critique or second-guess. He'll never really know what's going on with a team.

"I could see him retiring early. I don't see him managing until he's sixty-five or seventy. He'll enjoy life. Hang out in Venezuela. Do things here, do things there."

Guillen says he likes the good things in life because of his poor upbringing.

"I hope I die poor," he said, smiling. "I'm going to live rich to die poor. If my wife finds another boyfriend, he's gonna have to fucking work for it. If my kids want to be rich, they have to work. That's what I told my wife, 'I'm going to live rich and die poor. Who cares what happens after I die?' I ain't saving my money for my wife's boyfriend. She knows I'm right. I think my wife looks pretty hot. There's a lot of guys who want to go out with her and marry her. She's a good wife and good mom.

"But fuck it, if I like the car, I'll buy the car. I like this watch, I'll buy the watch. I like the house, I'll buy the house. Oh, what happened with the future? Future? I don't fucking know what my future's going to be. If I die rich, your boyfriend's going to have a lot of money.

"Everything I have that I own I love. I love everything I have around me because I know how much it cost. I know how lucky I am. If I like something, I get it. I told my wife, 'I never had these things.' It's why I teach my kids to appreciate what they have. Don't worry what you don't have. Just thank God for what you do have because there are people out there who have it worse than you do."

He used to be one of those people. He didn't have the family togetherness he wanted as a youngster. Now he does. But it takes work. It's not so different from being the manager of a major-league baseball team. Neither is it pain-free. You think you have a World Series–caliber team to start the season, and then Adam Dunn hits .159 and strikes out 177 times.

You think everything is fine at home, until it isn't.

You think you have found family with the White Sox until you realize you haven't and that you need to go somewhere else.

"People think that as soon as I leave the ballpark, everything's beautiful," Guillen said. "I've got a family. I've got problems. I've got a lot of shit, like everybody else. If you've got a wife, you've got a problem. If you have kids, you have problems. If you have a house, you have a problem. Everything in this motherfucking life is a problem. You've got to overcome those problems to be able to smile a little bit. Taxes. Dues. Sending a kid to college. This life? It's a fucked-up life."

If you've got a general manager, you've got a problem. If you've got players, you've got problems. Managing and parenting both cut into life expectancy. It's why mixing the two isn't always a good idea. But Guillen can't help himself.

Being the child of a professional baseball player often means having a long-distance relationship with your father. Extended absences are standard. And with night games, so are odd working hours. It can lead to children who hate their fathers, who hate baseball, or both.

As a player, Guillen worked hard at seeing his kids as much as possible. He often brought them to the ballpark. It led to his blowup with Terry Bevington. He wasn't going to let anyone or anything keep him from having what he didn't have as a child.

As a manager, he has taken the same approach, allowing his sons to hang out in the clubhouse and allowing players to bring their children to work as well. Ozzie Jr., who had been a color analyst for the White Sox' Spanish radio broadcasts, is a near-constant presence at his dad's home games. When Ozney was done with his high school or college season, he sometimes would work out with Sox players before games. Oney, who runs a marketing company with Ozzie Jr., was rarely seen in the Sox clubhouse after he resigned. That likely will change with the Marlins.

"My dad has tried so hard at marriage and being a father," Ozzie Jr. said. "He doesn't want to fail at it. That's why it's so important to him."

He is not going to let his job get in the way of his family. And his family is not going to get out of the way.

· 8 ·

PLAY THE ODDS

If this were the movie *Animal House*, Ozzie would be the Delta fraternity, whose members throw beer cans and food at photos of pledge candidates projected onto a wall. The Tony La Russas of the world would be the rich Omegas, whose initiation rites include solemn music and corporal-punishment paddling that the paddlers and the pledges seem to enjoy just a bit too much.

Hours before each game, Guillen walks into his office and finds a scouting report for that day's opponent resting neatly on his desk. Most of the time, he throws it straight into the garbage.

When the Sox were about to play the Angels in May 2011, he talked about the difference between him and his counterpart in Anaheim, Mike Scioscia.

"He weighs two hundred pounds more than me," he said, laughing. "He's bald, I'm not. He reads the scouting report, I don't. He has his own way."

During games, TV cameras often zoom in on managers

and coaches hunched over big books that look like school binders or family photo albums. The books contain hitter-pitcher matchup history, situational statistics, and other numbers that would make a stat freak throw away his Viagra.

Guillen views that collection of numbers the way he would the U.S. tax code—with glazed eyes. He has very little use for it. When it comes to stats, he usually goes cold turkey.

"I don't use anything," he said. "I swear to God. I don't make that shit up. The only stat I care about is winning and losing."

His philosophy is simple. What does a pile of stats know that he doesn't?

"If we're going to face fucking Detroit and I'm asking people for help, I'm a horseshit manager," he said. "I should know who we're facing every time for the last twenty years. With the National League, because I don't know the players, then we go by the scouting report a little bit more, or I read the scouting report more. Who's hot, who's not."

He's a gut guy who relies on experience and instincts. He takes into account what's inside a player's heart as much as what's in a player's statistical makeup. He wants to know how his hitter has been hitting lately, not how he has hit against a certain pitcher through the years.

Guillen will have to do a lot more studying in the National League, at least for a while. He'll see teams and players he hasn't seen much of in the past. He'll have to rely on the Marlins' advance scouts more than on his own two eyes. Joey Cora will be with him as his bench coach, but all that means is that they'll be together in the same boat. Sometimes that boat will be adrift.

Even when he has a scouting report in front him, Guillen

often is a skeptic. Numbers can tell half-truths. Let's say he had wanted to match Sox reliever Jesse Crain against Detroit's top slugger Miguel Cabrera.

"I can say, 'How's Cabrera against Crain?'" Guillen said. "But that doesn't mean anything. He can be 0-for-12 against Crain, but now Cabrera gets a base hit and now he's fucking 1-for-13 and the game's over.

"The first thing I think about is how's my guy throwing or how's my guy hitting. If my fucking guy's hitting good, why the fuck am I going to bring in a pinch hitter? You tell me he's 0-for-20 against this particular pitcher. Fuck that, I *know* my guy's been hitting good lately. I've been watching."

Guillen is not allergic to modern-day baseball sensibilities. He knows the sabermetrics approach has worked and that there are statistics that can help give a fuller picture of a player or a situation. But he thinks people sometimes get lost in numbers, to the point where a search party is required to find them.

"Somebody says, 'Oh, the guy who's coming to the plate for the other team is hitting .190 against lefties,'" Guillen said. "Well, how many lefties has he faced? Who has he faced? Or they say, 'He hits .600 against lefties.' Okay, what lefties? Fucking badass lefties like Sale or Thornton? No? Well, fuck him. You have to know the hitters. That's the pitcher he's going to have to face."

It's not surprising that the iconoclastic Guillen refuses to go by the book at times. It'd be a shocker if he did do things the way the cookie-cutter managers did things. Would it be safer? Of course it would be. But it wouldn't be Ozzie.

So going by what the book says about matchups? Guillen wags a finger of warning.

"Matchups are overrated, unless you're in the playoffs or in the World Series," he said. "When you're in our division, sooner or later you're going to face a guy. I hope [when we play Detroit] we don't have to face Verlander. But I'll bet you he'll be the first one we're going to face.

"A lot of people have different opinions about matchups. When you throw the ball good, I don't care who you're going to face. When you're struggling, I don't care who you face. When you're hitting, they can bring anybody in [to pitch], you're going to hit. I don't believe in matchups that much."

In a series against the Tigers in late July 2011, Guillen decided to pitch to the dangerous Cabrera rather than walk him. It paid off, with Cabrera failing to reach base. In another game, he walked Cabrera to pitch to another dangerous hitter, Victor Martinez, who also failed to reach base. Ozzie was 2-for-2 and feeling good about himself. A third time, he decided to pitch to Cabrera, who got a base hit to right field to help give his team a victory.

"That's the game," Guillen said. "It's gut and hope."

And bad decisions, too. On August 31, Ozzie brought in the hopelessly slumping Adam Dunn to pinch-hit for Brent Lillibridge against Twins closer Joe Nathan with men on second and third and the Sox trailing 7–4 in the ninth. This was the same Dunn whom Guillen had finally benched a few days before. And this was the same Lillibridge who already had a home run in the game. For good measure, this was also the Lillibridge who was 1-for-1 lifetime against Nathan. That one hit had been a home run.

The reaction at the Cell was one of disbelief. Disbelief quickly gave way to angry boos. And it wasn't just furious Sox fans who questioned the decision.

As Dunn prepared to come to the plate, Ozzie Jr. tweeted, "no, don't do it please don't do it why why why."

And . . .

"for the first time all season I don't agree with this move at all. Don't get it."

Ozzie Jr. later said his tweet was driven by the painful certainty that his dad was about to get heaped with abuse.

Dunn struck out swinging, which, considering he was hitting .163 and had already struck out 156 times, seemed almost preordained.

"Dunn can do a lot of things," Guillen said afterward. "I didn't like the matchup, Nathan against Lilli. Dunn can go up there and hit the ball out of the ballpark or walk. Obviously, he struck out, but that's the matchup I liked the best. Unfortunately, it didn't work."

Most people, if they're honest with themselves, don't think they can hit major-league pitching. But most every baseball fan thinks he can be a manager or, thanks to the proliferation of fantasy leagues, a general manager.

Because Guillen's personality is oversized, his in-game managing tends to get overlooked. He's a smart manager with a sharp intellect and a very good memory. Reinsdorf has said Guillen has the brightest baseball mind of anyone he knows. But because he's more of a "hunch" manager than a by-the-book manager, the people who regard the position the way others regard a Yale professorship tend to downgrade him.

The truth is that in a 162-game season, a manager has very little impact on the outcome of many games via strategy. People don't want to hear that because they prefer the image of the crafty skipper using his superior baseball acumen to outwit his opponent.

"As far as a strategist, it's not so much that Ozzie's underappreciated," Paul Konerko said. "I think in a lot of ways, strategy is probably overrated with the guys who get the credit for it. A lot of times in baseball, there are some moves here and there that get made and you're like, 'Okay, wow, that was pretty good.' But the game kind of plays itself. If you know a righty's coming up second in the eighth, well, a righty's up in the pen. You know what I mean? There are a lot of things that people get credit for being a genius about, but honestly it kind of plays itself out if you've been around the game handling players day to day.

"I'm sure way back when, the manager was who he was, and the players just had to adjust to him, period, or they were gone. Now the manager has to know a bunch of different personalities, know how to handle guys. You can't talk to this guy like this, but you can talk to that guy like that. Ozzie's pretty good at that. That's the biggest thing in the big leagues now."

As Konerko also points out, it helps if your manager played shortstop ten years or more in the big leagues. The whole coach-on-the-field concept fits a shortstop perfectly. He's the one who has had it ingrained in his head that he has to know everything that's happening on the field. He has to be ready for all eventualities. He has to be thinking ahead. There's no faking it.

Even when it comes to strategy, Guillen says, the secret to being a good manager is the ability to trust people—in this case, his coaches.

"I don't worry about who's pitching and who's not," he said. "I ask my coaches, can we run on him? He throws a slider, changeup, fastball. Can he throw a strike so we can hit-and-run?

That's all I care. Everything else, I let [the hitting coach] worry about that shit.

"Some managers try to cover every fucking thing, and at the end of the day, they don't cover shit. They want to talk to the hitter about hitting. They want to talk to the pitcher about pitching. They want to have a meeting about games. At the end of the day, you don't fucking know what you're doing.

"I let my coaches do what they're supposed to do. I pull the trigger. I accept suggestions, but it's my fucking call."

Guillen wants his coaches to disagree with him if they believe he's wrong. He wants them to question his decisions. Otherwise, he'd be the Hugo Chavez of baseball. There already are enough dictators in the game.

It's one thing for a manager to say he wants his coaches to be outspoken when it comes to decisions. It's another for them to be outspoken. The manager has the coaches' fate in his hands. It takes a strong person to disagree with the boss.

Guillen said it happens all the time on his staff.

"Hell, yes," he said. "Me and [Sox pitching coach Don Cooper] fight every fucking minute of the day. At the end of the day, I explain to him why I'm doing something. They've changed my mind before—if you give me the right fucking reason. I want to give you mine."

For example, Cooper wanted to give reliever Hector Santiago a chance in 2011. The White Sox had finally called up Santiago in early June after he had spent five years in the minors. But the club was trying to fight its way back into contention after its miserable start, and Guillen was in no mood to pitch Santiago just to make him feel good. By early July, the right-hander had made only two appearances. This wasn't a time for nurturing. This was a time for winning.

"Every day, we're down by one run or two runs," Guillen said. "I don't want to fucking put that kid in. I want to give my team the best shot for the night. Coop wanted him in. I didn't put him in. Maybe if we're down by seven runs tomorrow, then we'll pitch him.

"But if you don't trust your coaches and you don't listen to what they say, then what the fuck do you have coaches for?"

When all is said and done, in-game decisions rest with the manager and nobody else. He's the one who makes the call, and he's the one who sweats it out while the decision is very much in doubt. He's the one who's going to get second-guessed. No matter how decisive Guillen might be, he's tense while he waits to see if his move will work or not.

In a game against Detroit on July 25, Carlos Quentin singled to left in the seventh inning. Guillen brought in Lillibridge to pinch-run for Quentin. That way, he'd have more speed on the bases and a better right fielder in the game in the later innings, when defense could be crucial. But it came with a very big risk. The Sox were leading 6–3, and Guillen was hoping that his bullpen would keep the game out of reach and that he wouldn't be hurt by not having one of his best hitters, Quentin, in the game.

He knew that if the Tigers came back, there was a decent chance Lillibridge would come to the plate in the ninth inning. If the Sox lost, the abuse Guillen would take for not having Quentin at the plate in the ninth would be immense.

The gamble paid off. The Sox won, and Guillen didn't have to kick himself for taking Quentin out of a game against a team they were chasing. But he did struggle with the decision—briefly.

"I go, 'We're facing fucking Detroit,'" he said. "Then I said,

'Ah, fuck it, bringing Lillibridge in late in games is what we've done all year long.' You roll the dice. But I always can sleep at night. If that works or doesn't work, fuck you, everybody. I don't give a shit. But if you don't do something you wanted to do and things don't go your way, you say, 'Fuck, why didn't I do that?' "

This sets Ozzie off on another of his favorite topics: how baseball's rules on substitutions are so much more restrictive than those in other sports. Let's see if New England Patriots coach Bill Belichick would be considered a genius when a player he takes out can't come back into the game, Guillen says.

"I wish when somebody struggled I could say, 'Okay, this guy's going to hit for you, but you're going to go back in the field,' " he said. "When I make one move, that guy can't go back in the field. Basketball, football, all those sports, those [coaches] can do more with the lineups. I see a couple guys with the Bulls that as soon as the fourth period comes around, they take their shoes off because they can't play defense. I wish I could do that. We can't. If you're good on defense and you're terrible on offense, you can make one move, that's it."

It's why decisions feel heavier for baseball managers. Guillen might be able to sleep at night, but when he's in the middle of a game, he can be all raw nerve endings. A lot goes into every decision. A lot of emotion gets spent waiting to see if it's the right one. A July 2011 road game against the Cubs captured the tension.

Joey Cora approached Guillen to tell him that Jesse Crain, who was going to pitch the bottom of the eighth inning with a 6–4 Sox lead, would be batting third in the top of the ninth. Guillen's preference was to pitch Crain in both the eighth and the ninth because Sergio Santos, the closer, had pitched the previous two days, picking up saves in both games, and might not be sharp three days in a row. Ozzie thought the biggest issue would be in letting Crain hit.

He was wrong about that.

"Crain throws nineteen pitches in the eighth inning, and we're dying in the dugout," Guillen said. "And nobody appreciates that. We're praying for a guy to make the play on a ground ball because I want Crain for the next inning. People don't know that shit."

Because Crain's pitch count was so high, Guillen pinch-hit for him in the top of the ninth and brought in Santos to close. Santos picked up the save. It wasn't how Ozzie planned it, but he didn't turn it down. The next day, he used Matt Thornton in the eighth and the ninth in a 1–0 victory. The bullpen got a rest and Guillen was able to breathe again.

For a manager, there's strategy and there's knowledge. Two different things. Strategy is knowing what to do during games. Knowledge is using everything that's at your disposal to make those decisions. One of the quirks of U.S. Cellular Field is that the indoor batting cages sit between the White Sox clubhouse and their dugout. There aren't cages specifically for the visiting team's use. Before games, opposing players have to walk through the Chicago dugout to use the cages. During games, White Sox players can use them, but their opponents can't. It means that one team can get potential pinch hitters warmed up, the other can't.

It played a role in how Guillen used his bullpen.

"I'm more careful about switching pitchers on the road because the other team has a fucking cage, and they've been hitting," he said. "Here, I bring the pitcher in because they can't hit. They don't have a cage there. They can't get loose. At other parks, this team's got a cage, that team's got a cage. They've been hitting for a little while. They're going to be loose. At our ballpark? Fuck. Fuck you. You come from the bench, you beat me from the bench."

Ozzie will have to find an edge somewhere else. The new Marlins ballpark has separate batting cages for the visiting team.

Just like every other manager, Guillen sometimes makes bad decisions. But he likes to think he makes them for the right reasons.

In another game against the Tigers, Guillen walked to the mound to see how right-hander Philip Humber was feeling. Humber had been a revelation for the White Sox in the first half of the 2011 season, going 8–5 with a 3.10 earned-run average. If it hadn't been for his success early in the season, Guillen's team might have fallen apart for good.

The Sox were winning 3–1 when Victor Martinez, a switch-hitter, came to the plate with men on second and third. Martinez was hitting .270 from the right side and .330 from the left. Guillen could have pulled Humber for a left-hander, to force Martinez to bat righty. He could have had Humber intentionally walk Martinez. But Humber told his manager he felt fine, and that was all Guillen needed to hear. He would let Humber pitch to Martinez, batting lefty.

This time the approach didn't work. Martinez singled to right field, driving in two runs to tie the game.

"He gave me the right answer, wrong result," Guillen said.

It's fair to say most managers would have yanked a fairly inexperienced pitcher in that spot. Everything about the situation called for making Martinez bat from the right side. But

Guillen was more interested in building up Humber than he was in doing the "right" thing. Was it ill-advised? The result said it was. He had done the same thing with Humber earlier in the season and paid the price then, too.

It was very similar to the situation Guillen had confronted in June with a struggling Sergio Santos on the mound. And Guillen again thought the reward—a young pitcher who would gain confidence by knowing his manager believed in him—was worth any risk. Given a choice, he'll sometimes go with emotion over wonkish reasoning. It frustrates the people who view baseball as a poetic math equation.

He brought Chris Sale into a game against Oakland in April, hoping the hard-throwing young reliever could pick up a save less than twenty-four hours after he had thrown thirty-four pitches in two innings the night before. Sale proceeded to give up a double and two singles before Guillen came out to get him.

"[We had a] three-run lead, and he said he could go," Guillen said afterward.

That game was educational for another reason. It showed how sensitive Ozzie can be when questioned about his decisions. It was the game that would make him declare afterward, "We have no closer."

"When we play good, they send those guys to this goddamn table and [reporters] talk to them like heroes," he said in the postgame press conference. "When we fuck it up, I'm the one who has to goddamn sit here and talk to you guys."

But give Guillen this: he's consistent. When his team plays well, he credits his players. When it doesn't, he normally blames himself. Every once in a while, though, he lashes out when the team has made one of his decisions look bad.

Being considered a player's manager can be a good thing,

but it often comes with an unpleasant tag attached: Not a Good Strategist. Guillen is touchy about this, though he insists he doesn't care.

In a game against the Cubs at the end of June, he decided to leave right-handed reliever Brian Bruney on the mound, rather than bring in Will Ohman, a lefty, to face Blake DeWitt and Kosuke Fukudome, both of whom hit left-handed. Why? With the Sox up by two runs, he said, Fukudome represented only the tying run. And after him, the Cubs would have three right-handed hitters coming to the plate.

"That's fucking good managing," Guillen said.

Bruney struck out both batters.

A day earlier, he had sent Juan Pierre from first on a hit-and-run in the first inning. If he hadn't, it would have been a likely double play. The Sox ended up getting two runs in the inning. Guillen might not be a big stats guy, but he does look at them once in a while.

"You know why I try to do [hit-and-runs] more often? We lead the league in ground ball double plays," he said. "I say, 'Fuck it, I've got to send those guys.' "

Guillen is excited about being unleashed on the National League, if for no other reason than to have a chance to strategize more and to show off his managing chops.

In the American League, you make out your lineup with a designated hitter, and you never have to worry about double switches, whether your pitcher is going to bunt or swing away, or how much longer you can use your pitcher because his spot in the batting order is coming up. An American League manager flips the cruise-control switch and watches the game. He doesn't have to worry as much about the pitching element the way a National League manager does.

"People in the stands don't understand what we go through here," he said during the 2011 season. "The other day I said I'd rather be in the National League than the American League. The first thing everybody says, 'Oh, he wants to go to the Marlins.' No. As a manager, it's more fun for me—don't bring this guy in or we can't pinch hit for him because it's only the third inning. In the American League, you just sit there and say, 'Okay, get Thornton up in the bullpen.'"

It's why Guillen looked forward to interleague games in his eight years with the White Sox. He believes that to win in the National League, a team has to have a good bullpen and three good utility players whom a manager can use like chess pieces.

A few days after the Sox had beaten the Rockies in an interleague game in Denver, he was still like a kid in a candy store. He hadn't been able to use a designated hitter because it was a road game in a National League city. Free at last.

"I moved Teahen from right field to first base, then first base to third base," he said. "Nobody knows that shit. Then we move him back to right field because we don't have Quentin [who had already pinch-hit]. I like that shit. In the American League, it's like okay, 'This guy runs for Quentin and goes to the outfield.' Fucking boring."

If you turn on a sports talk radio station after a game in any baseball town, you'll hear fans criticizing the manager for the sorry state of his critical-thinking skills. If you listen long enough, you'll hear different fans offering drastically different solutions to the same decision. They all think their answer is the correct one. What they agree on is that the manager seems to have his head up his ass, which is making it very difficult for him to see the game. That's the beauty of baseball. Anyone who played Little League thinks he knows more than the manager.

If he could, Guillen would let fans, reporters, and other assorted know-it-alls manage for a few innings.

"I guarantee if I put any of you out here during a game, you wouldn't know what to do," he told reporters one day. "I did it to Peter Gammons. I said, 'Peter, you think you know about baseball? Sit next to me, motherfucker, and manage this spring-training game.' When you guys are in the third inning, my mind's in the sixth already: 'If this happens, this guy's coming back, who do we have available?' It goes fast, very fast. I'm Chicago tough because I don't care if people second-guess me or not. That's baseball. That's why baseball has so many fans, just because they think they can manage."

Every once in a while, Guillen likes to go against convention. In Chicago, it had energized him, made him feel as if he was doing something in a league that didn't allow a manager as many opportunities to think and react. It probably won't come as a surprise that he's not averse to making the grand statement. In 2010, he went with a designated-hitter-by-committee. The Sox had decided not to re-sign Jim Thome, their primary designated hitter in 2009, and Guillen saw an opportunity to get away from the typical profile of the DH as a power hitter who couldn't hit for average.

He gets points for imagination and demerits for results. The DH committee of Mark Kotsay, Paul Konerko, Juan Pierre, Carlos Quentin, Alex Rios, and Mark Teahen ranked ninth out of fourteen American League teams in on-base percentage (.332) and slugging percentage (.396), and tenth in home runs (18) for designated hitters. Then again, it was leaps and bounds beyond what Adam Dunn would offer the Sox the next season.

In the end, neither Ozzie nor Kenny could say they were right when it came to the DH.

In 2011, Guillen made a move that isn't seen often in the big leagues. The Sox went to a six-man pitching rotation. It was born of necessity and the suspicion that Jake Peavy couldn't make it through an entire season unless compromises were made or some new drug were invented that healed injuries instantly.

Peavy had had surgery in July 2010 to repair a detached latissimus dorsi, which had occurred nine days before while he was delivering a pitch. It was an injury few pitchers have experienced and fewer have recovered from. The Sox wanted to take a conservative approach to his recovery in 2011, knowing that the gung ho Peavy likely would need to be saved from himself.

On May 18, in his second start since the surgery, Peavy pitched a three-hitter against Cleveland. Over the previous year, Peavy had been through a lot and had put the Sox through a lot, to the point where no one was counting on him for much more than another dashed hope or two. He had become the Boy Who Cried "I'm Healthy!" But his victory brought on some optimism, though a wary strain of it.

Did Ozzie truly trust that Peavy was healed for good? No. A few weeks earlier, he had been asked when he would consider Peavy healthy. His answer was "next year." Guillen did trust that his pitcher was as passionate as he was about winning. He couldn't do much about Peavy's fragility, but he loved his competitiveness.

He couldn't count on him, though, leading to the decision to go with a six-man rotation of Mark Buehrle, John Danks, Gavin Floyd, Edwin Jackson, Philip Humber, and Peavy. It worked from May 11 to June 25. The Sox went 24–17.

What do they say about all the best intentions? The idea was to get the pitchers some rest, especially Peavy. He eventually was shut down because of arm fatigue. Humber and Danks had stints on the disabled list.

"We do everything for them," Guillen said. "We shuffle one thing to another to make sure those guys are feeling strong. I don't think Coop, myself [should be blamed]. Any doubts we didn't do the right thing for them to finish strong are wrong because we did. We had many meetings about that situation because in the past Buehrle kind of tended to wear down a little bit [at the end of a season], Gavin, the way Peavy was. Humber never threw that many innings in the big leagues. We did the right thing for them to finish strong. . . . We thought we were going to be in a pennant race all the way to the end and thought it would help them."

The problem with a six-man rotation, as Guillen found out, was that it taxed his bullpen. In a game against Toronto, the Sox went into extra innings, and Guillen was forced to bring in Floyd as a reliever.

With his team dead in the water in late September, Guillen wasn't feeling good about much. Doubt had crept into his thoughts and, once there, had made the predictable journey to his tongue.

"It makes you wonder if you're managing well, if my coaching staff did their job," he said. "I wonder about a lot of things. Was it the right thing to go with a six-man rotation? Did we do the right thing to keep Dunn and Rios in the lineup? All this stuff. It's so much tougher when you have a losing season. A lot of people suffered here from the top to the bottom. I can take the blame. I don't make excuses because they give me a good ball club. Why we don't play well is people's opinion. We don't play the way we should, and I take blame with that."

Where is Guillen's place as a tactician in the hierarchy of managers? You don't do what he has done with a limited intellect. You don't win a World Series, be named Manager of the Year, and in essence get traded to another team for two minor-league players without the ability to manage a game.

But people get wrapped up in his entertainment value and can't see the forest for the tee-hees. They see a man who can command a crowd, who is fearless with his opinions, but can't see the manager who is always thinking ahead during a game. And it bothers him. Sometimes he forces the issue to show that he can think on his feet, to fight against the perception of him as a player's manager and not a manager's manager.

Critics surely will look at his habit of throwing away the scouting report without a glance before most games as proof he's hopelessly stuck in an era when managers got by on vague hunches and feelings. Guillen is not opposed to statistical analysis. He thinks it has its place. Sue him for believing its place shouldn't be at the forefront of the game.

In a way, he's a victim of his own personality. And the first Venezuelan manager in major-league history has had to fight the stereotype of the fiery Latino who thinks with his heart and not with his head.

An irresponsible manager would come to a new team and a new league and think he doesn't need to do his homework. Guillen knows he's going to have to learn the National League the way he did the American League. But in the end, the game is still about players, and Ozzie knows that managers win because of the talent they are given. He believes that how he treats his players as men—with encouragement and faith—is the truest indicator of a good manager. Numbers and strategy are secondary.

"Last year at the winter meetings, I see Bobby Cox, Lou Piniella, and Cito Gaston," he said. "I want to be those guys one day. I want to sit there retired. Good managers and good players retire. Horseshit managers and horseshit players get fired."

If you ask him whether he wants to be considered among the game's best managers, he is quick with an answer. It doesn't mean it's the real answer, but it's the one he offers up for public consumption.

"I don't care," he said. "I don't. I was talking with my family about this. That's not what I'm looking for. I'm looking to win games and to make sure the players give me respect. What's out there? I'm only going to be a good manager when I've got like two thousand wins. Right now, I don't look at that."

Heading into the 2012 season with the Marlins, Guillen's managerial record was 678–617. He knows that whatever it will be when he leaves Miami will depend heavily on the quality of players the Marlins bring in. The team he inherited finished thirty games out of first place in the National League East.

He could turn into a strategic genius, and it won't matter a bit if a player has a disastrous season like the one Dunn had in 2011. Maybe another manager would have been able to bring Dunn out of his tailspin. Nobody will ever know.

The danger of painting Guillen as a showman more than a manager is that it turns him into a caricature. And it leaves no room for giving him his due as a person who pays attention to detail. When the Sox were struggling offensively early in the season, Guillen moved Konerko from cleanup to third in the order. The Sox couldn't seem to get a hit in the first inning, and Guillen grew tired of seeing Konerko lead off the second inning. The idea is to get your best hitters as many at-bats as possible, right?

If the embellishers' image of Guillen is correct—that he seems more concerned with making outrageous statements than with managing—then he wouldn't have been alert enough to make even such a small move.

When he steps back and looks at it, he takes a very Ozzie-like self-improvement approach.

"Lineups don't make good hitters," he said. "They've got to go out and perform. I don't believe in who's protecting who, who's there, who's behind, who's leading off. When you're hot, you're hot. When you're not, you're not. I just keep making lineups that I think are the best ones and hopefully those guys start performing."

Guillen has a dream. If we were to put him on a couch and interpret it, we might say it stems from his deep desire to be recognized for his baseball mind. In his fantasy, he brings in a right-handed reliever to pitch to a right-handed hitter. When the pitcher gets the out, Guillen walks to the mound to make a pitching change, but instead of sending the pitcher to the dugout, he tells him to replace the right fielder. He motions for the center fielder to move closer to right field as insurance. He brings in a lefty to face the next batter, a left-handed hitter. When his pitcher strikes him out with some 98 mph heat—hey, he dreams big—Guillen walks to the mound, sends the lefty to the dugout, and motions for his new right fielder to pitch again to the right-handed hitters who will be coming to the plate.

This way, he has burned through only one pitcher, instead of two, and has given his bullpen a break. In his dream, a ball does not get hit down the right-field line, nor does his reliever strain a hamstring running after it.

If the narrator in this dream says that it takes a bright mind to make such a bold decision, Ozzie will not disagree.

"I will make that move before my career is over as a manager," he declares.

Before the 2011 season began, Guillen stood in a hallway inside the White Sox' spring-training facility in Glendale, Arizona. The topic was whether a manager is ever truly appreciated. The answer, typically, was about that and more.

"Put it this way, I have respect for every manager," he said. "When I won Manager of the Year, the trophy was sitting in my office for almost a year. Listen, I'd rather have a ring than twenty Manager of the Year awards. Just give me one more ring. Manager of the Year—that's overrated. That's overrated. I see a lot of Managers of the Year get fired.

"Who's the best manager in baseball? [Minnesota's] Ron Gardenhire. He's better than me for so many reasons. I'm not looking to be called the best manager. I'm looking for that next ring and to manage as long as I can."

By the end of the season, he would be singing a decidedly different tune about the value of World Series rings.

· 9 ·

MANAGE UP

It was the end of August 2011, and Kenny Williams was sitting in the seats behind home plate as the White Sox were going through batting practice at the Cell. They were preparing to play the Minnesota Twins that evening, but their general manager, with some prodding, was thinking back to Ozzie Guillen's first interview for the Sox manager's job in 2003, the one in which Ozzie showed up hungover.

"I made the decision to hire him in the midst of an argument," Williams said. "I said, 'What makes you think, with me knowing who you are and your type of personality, that I'm going to put you in charge of the Chicago White Sox?' And he took great offense to it. He stood up and said, 'Well, why the fuck did you bring me here if you don't think I can do it? You know me. What the fuck do you want? Do you want a fucking team that gets after it and respects the game?' He continued on from there."

Business schools don't generally recommend dropping F-bombs during job interviews. It's not considered the traditional path to choice management positions. And even Guillen, whose vulgarity is second nature, must have believed on some level that he was talking his way out of a job. In reality, he was talking his way into one. Williams liked that Ozzie had the guts to say what he felt. The best decisions often come out of open dialogue, not out of total surrender to the boss's opinion.

But what Williams took away from that interview, and what he was thinking about almost eight years later as he watched batting practice, was the concept of a package deal. He had hired all of Guillen—the bright mind, the outspoken leader, the bundle of joy, and the man who could cause as much agony as the worst toothache. Pleasure and pain—that's Ozzie.

Williams knew he couldn't pick and choose with Guillen. It's not a cafeteria line. He couldn't embrace the part of Ozzie that helped him win a World Series in 2005 and reject the parts he didn't like when things went poorly.

Whenever Ozzie started a fire, Williams knew he couldn't say he was having trouble recognizing the man he had hired. It was the same man who had stood up and cursed in a job interview. That part of Guillen had thrilled Williams eight years before.

"Same guy, same person," Williams said. "People ask me often how I can put up with this or that. I tell them, 'I know who I hired.' I never asked him not to be the man that he is. I have asked him on occasion to use the words 'no comment,' and he basically told me that was impossible. I said, 'Well, since you can't use those words, would you just be mindful of the impact that your words have and the potential for them to be to the detriment of the team and to yourself?' "

Williams's pet saying for how he dealt with the commotion Guillen caused with his mouth had to do with self-survival: "I'm not necessarily too busy to hear all the stuff, but I'm certainly too busy to pay much attention to it." In other words, if you allow yourself to get caught up in Ozzie's turbulence, it's your own fault.

If that's the case, Williams could blame himself for some of their problems early on. He approached his job the way a football coach might. He preferred that a cone of silence be clamped over the organization. He believed in good appearances.

Guillen, of course, was the opposite. Williams learned to take an it's-never-boring-around-here approach to Ozzie and his outbursts. But that changed, too, as the incidents piled up.

"It used to be entertaining," Williams said as he watched batting practice. "It's not so much fun anymore. I'm just being honest. It's not so much fun anymore."

Unbeknownst to Williams, on the very same day he was contemplating the various sides of Guillen, the manager was talking with Joe Cowley of the *Chicago Sun-Times*, whose column the next day would quote a source as saying the Ozzie-Kenny relationship was "beyond repair." Cowley also reported that the White Sox had begun "getting a feel" for managerial candidates and had renewed talks with the Marlins about compensation for Guillen should he go to Florida to manage. By this, Cowley implied, Williams had been doing the reaching out.

All the things about Williams that frustrated Guillen flared up: the fact that most of Guillen's coaches didn't have contracts for 2012 and were living lives of doubt and anxiety; that the manager had taken the lion's share of criticism for a disappointing season; that the Sox hadn't handled the Ozney draft situation well; that perhaps Jerry Reinsdorf had finally had enough of the Ozzie-Kenny soap opera and had settled on Williams as the last man standing.

"I can leave Chicago with my head up," Ozzie told Cowley.

The next day, with reporters huddled around him, Guillen talked about wanting a contract extension. He was under contract through 2012, but managing that season without a new deal would make him a lame duck. He said he wouldn't come back without an extension.

"We deserve more," he said.

What was the managerial purpose of this? A few people argued that this was Ozzie again trying to take pressure off of his team, but it rang hollow. What pressure? The team was hovering just above .500 and was six games out of first place. The Ozzie-as-motivator theory was a weak positive spin on a bad situation. The critics were saying that Guillen's selfishness was showing through, that with his team in a pennant race, he had chosen to talk about money and his future. But in reality, this was Guillen's insecurity showing through. For all his bravado, he's a man in need of love. And he hadn't been feeling much of it during the season.

The topic of Ozzie as a distraction would come up four days later after the Sox had lost to the Detroit Tigers and Justin Verlander. Guillen sounded wounded by the idea that his demand for a contract extension was disruptive.

"The people out there think this is going be a distraction in the pennant? Fuck them," he said. "It's not a distraction. If people think we're horseshit because I made that comment, fuck them, too. I respect my players more than anything. I will never do something to hurt my players or make a distraction for my players. I don't get a DUI. I don't get caught doing something stupid. I just got caught doing what? Answer a question people ask me? No. Is that a distraction? No, Verlander was a distraction. They've been playing for me for eight years. You think they care? If the people out there think that, fuck them."

Later that day, the Tigers would come back from an 8–1 deficit to beat the White Sox 9–8. The next day, they clobbered the Sox 18–2 for the sweep. Any thoughts the Sox might have entertained of winning the division were gone.

It's impossible to know whether the latest chapter in the ongoing saga of Ozzie Guillen had distracted his team. But the question was there for anyone to take a swing at.

"I don't think in a situation where you are trying to make a move to first place or second place . . . you really want to hear stuff coming out about managers' contracts or anybody being involved in any kind of contract," Omar Vizquel said. "I think everybody was pretty focused on the job that we needed to do on the field. Most of the guys here are veteran players, mature, and I don't think that could be some kind of distraction. . . . But obviously you needed to focus on the baseball side."

Guillen's public request for a contract extension was another salvo in his ongoing battle with Williams. It really was about Guillen's need for security in the face of his insecurities about his general manager. He didn't want to be left hanging in 2012.

A distraction? It's impossible to quantify. But at a minimum, the Ozzie-Kenny dynamic had not always been entertaining for the players.

"I'm pretty much like everybody who's got a part to play

here as far as doing your best for the team, doing your job to make a winning team," Paul Konerko had said earlier in the season. "Anything else that's not part of that is a deterrent to winning. If you ask me if I was a fan of watching all that, the answer is, anything that's outside of what is the job tonight and for the season and can be a drag on that, I don't like."

What about the turmoil caused by the Oney Guillen situation in 2010?

"I don't like any of it," Konerko said. "Do I think it has an effect? That's up for debate. I don't think anybody can ever answer that."

What Guillen has never comprehended—and bless him for it—is that he doesn't have to answer every question with raw honesty. Saying something with nuance is not saying "no comment." The media love his openness. The Sox sometimes didn't. The contract-extension talk was one of those times when the team would have preferred something more tactful from him. Something along the lines of, "This is not the time to discuss my situation. Let's wait until after the season to see what happens."

But does that sound anything like Ozzie? No. It sounds like a corporate spokesman. And in truth, his approach made some sense, at least for him. The Marlins job would not be open forever. It would be much better if he knew what the Sox' intentions were.

On the day Cowley's *Sun-Times* column came out, Williams wasn't quite as introspective as he had been while watching batting practice the day before. When reporters asked about Ozzie's future with the club, his response was blunt.

"If I'm asked that question one more time, I'm going to throw up," Williams said.

Guillen then followed his traditional binge-and-purge pattern. After having his say about his contract situation, he went into play-nice mode. He said he got along with Williams better than any other manager gets along with his general manager. He said he wasn't upset. He said he could work with Williams going forward.

Huh?

"I don't see why not," he said. "We played together and we grew up in the organization. I don't think [Tigers manager] Jim Leyland is hugging and having a drink with the general manager [Dave Dombrowski]. They work together. They work for the team. We're still good friends, not great friends like we were. But we can [work together]. And I am a good manager, even if people don't think I am. Cocky and arrogant, but there are worse guys out there than me."

As much as Guillen wanted to paint a picture of a one-time strong friendship with Williams, they had never been close. It might have been another example of Ozzie, having vented, now overcompensating with a blue-sky view of the world.

"People might take this wrong," Ozzie Jr. said. "But if the general manager is Joey Cora or Harold Baines or Robin Ventura, I'd be like, 'Wow, the relationship has gone to shit.' Because they were his friends. They were close.

"I don't see why people think that my dad and Kenny were buddy-buddy. They were teammates, yeah. They have a relationship as boss–manager. Kenny hired him. I don't think the relationship in that aspect of general manager–manager has changed at all. It's two guys who have very similar attitudes when it comes to what they think. They're not going to hold back when they want to say something. They're both very passionate about the team.

"Do I think they're friends? No. Do I think [Yankees manager] Joe Girardi and [Yankees general manager] Brian Cashman go out and have dinner? Maybe for work. That doesn't mean they're friends."

Williams agreed.

"We'd hang out and go to dinner from time to time and shoot the breeze and stuff, but no, we weren't going to each other's kids' birthday parties and that kind of stuff," he said. "But we've known each other a long time. We've respected each other for a long time. I never lost sight of that."

Creative tension can be good in the business world and in baseball. So can conflict, as long as it's contained. Viewpoints are challenged. Under scrutiny, long-held procedures give way to new-and-improved procedures. But what happened in Chicago might or might not be instructive in Miami. It could be a cautionary tale, or it could be something the Marlins want to keep in mind, or it could be nothing more than a one-and-done personality clash.

The infighting between Williams and Guillen had been going on, in varying degrees, for at least three years, and although they had often gone back and forth like this in public, exhaustion seemed to have set in. With the backbiting at its worst, it was reasonable to ask whether they could still get along.

"I can definitely work with him," Williams said. "The only thing that's ever come into question is, there is a certain level of respect that you need to have, regardless of your personality and how your public perception is and how it needs to be fed. There still is a level of respect you have to have. As long as that's intact, I think we're okay because we can continue to talk about the betterment of the team. And we always have done that."

Which raised the obvious question: Was there still enough respect between the two men to have a productive working relationship? Williams's answer showed the disconnect.

"If there's not from his end, then he's done a damn good job of hiding it from me," he said. "I certainly think what's happening here [with the disappointing 2011 season], I take full responsibility. These guys are the same coaches that when I give them good teams, they've had people produce. Alex Rios should have been an All-Star in 2010. Nobody's going to be able to forget what he's doing now. Adam Dunn, same thing. Am I to place that on the manager's head if I know they're all working hard and giving the same effort that they always have been? I'm not doing that. In 2007, when we lost the most games under my tenure, I gave the coaches all contract extensions. I'll carry that weight for everyone. He doesn't need to carry it. I can carry the weight of disappointment, ridicule, and still do what I need to do to perform my job."

Sometimes mutual respect didn't seem to be anywhere in the vicinity of the two men. As the 2011 season wore on, Ozzie and his coaches fed off one another's worries. The Guillen side felt that Williams had changed after the Sox had won the World Series in 2005, that he had become full of himself. Some of the coaches didn't trust Williams. For his part, Williams was used to the turmoil but tired of it.

Whether he was trying to or not, Guillen seemed to be acting as the travel agent for his own departure. The Marlins wanted him. There was no doubt of that. They had hired the eighty-year-old Jack McKeon as their interim manager in June with an eye toward making another run at Guillen after the season. In 2010, after much agonizing, Ozzie had decided against going to Miami, saying his heart was in Chicago. The White Sox, in turn, had picked up his option for the 2012 season.

But now, in 2011, Guillen saw leverage. He wanted the Sox to pony up with a contract extension. The Marlins were likely to offer a multiyear deal. The Sox were scheduled to pay him $2.5 million in 2012 but had no obligation beyond that. If Guillen wanted to blame someone for his current contract, he could blame himself. He had negotiated it without an agent.

If the Sox wanted him, they would have to add more years to his contract, or so he believed. The downside? He didn't seem to want to go to the Marlins. The team would be moving into its new ballpark in 2012, but Miami was a baseball-forsaken city. The fans didn't care about the team, and they had shown it year after year with their absence at games. When the threat of Hurricane Irene forced the Marlins and the Cincinnati Reds to play a doubleheader on August 24, only 347 people showed up for the hastily scheduled first game, according to a fan who did a head count and tweeted it.

Guillen also didn't care much for the city of Miami. In late July and early August, he made several references to the poor attendance at Marlins games. He said there was a reason he bought a home in Chicago in 2010 and lived there rather than in his Miami off-season home.

"I moved from Miami because I think the people there are fake," he said.

"It's the fakest place in the world," Ozzie Jr. said.

Guillen would be the show with the Marlins, but it would be like playing summer stock in Poughkeepsie after his experience in Chicago, where he was a star. And he had deep roots with the White Sox. He had been with the organization as a player or manager for more than twenty years. If he went to Miami, he'd have the roots of seaweed.

"If you go manage another team, you've got no affiliation," Ozzie Jr. said in August. "They fire you, the team sucks, whatever. But he's always going to be associated with the White Sox."

As September wore on, Guillen talked more and more about wanting to stay in Chicago. When asked whether he would be willing to jettison one of his coaches if Reinsdorf demanded it, he didn't say no. For someone who had always backed his staff, it was a telling non-reply.

The Cubs were the elephant in the room. If Ozzie truly wanted to own Chicago, it would help if he were wearing a Cubs uniform. The city had always been split on its baseball loyalty, but starting in the early 1980s the Cubs began drawing huge crowds at Wrigley Field. Part of that had to do with the arrival of bigger-than-life TV announcer Harry Caray, who had moved from the South Side to the North Side. And part of it was the power of superstation WGN, which had brought in fans from all over the country. The Sox ended up being the poor cousin, and not even the World Series in 2005 and Guillen's big personality looked like it could change that.

But the Cubs started losing attendance in 2010. Fans appeared to finally be sick of the decades of futility. They began to show their displeasure by not showing up in the huge numbers they had before. The Cubs fired general manager Jim

Hendry in August 2011, and there was talk about the necessity of a culture change at Wrigley. What would be a bigger culture change for the cute-and-cuddly, PG-rated Cubs than an R-rated manager?

Some portion of White Sox fans had grown tired of Guillen's act and wanted the team to fire him, but how would they feel if he went to the archenemy?

Ozzie Jr. thought people had their eye on the wrong ball, the one with the Marlins insignia on it.

"I think it's funny that people think the Miami rumors are true," he said. "But anytime someone brings up the Cubs, that's when I'm like, Wow. That's the one I'm like . . . people don't think the Cubs would pull the trigger. That would be his decision. I don't know how he'd take it. But it would be a hard one to make because of the rivalry between the two teams. That's like you're a wrestler, and you go from being the hero, being Hulk Hogan, and then turning into a villain."

Guillen is smart enough to avoid insulting fans, and even when he does, as he did with his fans-pissing-on-statues comment earlier in the season, he's quick to deny it. But there was no doubt he was getting tired of the almost constant carping of the White Sox faithful. The 2011 season had been a frustrating one. A team with a huge payroll and expectations had failed. He and a lot of fans had thought the Sox were a possible World Series team. He was the guy sitting above the dunk tank.

For all of Ozzie's assertions during the season that he never paid attention to fans' responses on his Twitter account, he did. And they bothered him. He was used to Sox fans' tendency toward doom and gloom, but it wore on him. Even during the

2005 season, when the Sox went on to win a championship, fans saw disaster around every corner. Like the Cubs, the Sox had gone through a long dry spell when it came to World Series titles, their previous one having come in 1917. Their fans had trust issues.

Toward the end of 2011, Guillen finally admitted what everybody already knew anyway: he does listen to public opinion.

"The only way I read papers is if Joey Cora tells me, 'You should read this,'" he said. "My mind is on Mexican soap opera, Venezuelan news—my mind's not on baseball. When I get here, yes. Reading the paper and what people say, I just laugh. I hear a couple radio shows because when I go home and come back, I want to know what they're saying. But I don't mind. On my Twitter yesterday, everybody was killing me. How terrible I was, that Viciedo should have been here two years ago, before he came to the United States. That's the way it is. That's why you're the manager. You have to take the blame. You have to take it like a man."

But Guillen had to listen to the loud complaints of fans who sat near the White Sox dugout at the Cell. They wanted him to do something, anything, for God's sake. He had to listen to callers on the postgame radio show to find out how bad a manager he was. It was getting old, even if he wasn't admitting that publicly.

But the alternative—a quieter city with more patient, less passionate fans—was not a good match for Guillen, and he knew it. He laughed about how docile the crowds were in some of the smaller markets, especially Seattle. He needed to be wherever it was messy, where life came with sharp edges. And even then, he'd make it messier and sharper.

"I always tell him, 'This is Chicago. This is a sports town. If you go somewhere else, it'll get real boring real quick real easy,' " Ozzie Jr. said. "I know our fans can be mean and rude and all of the above sometimes, but I can't say anything bad because I'm like that with the Bears. I boo the crap out of them. That's just how Chicago is."

The phrase "managing up" means to go beyond your job duties in a way that enhances your supervisor's work and helps reach goals that are important to both of you. Or it can mean being a major brown nose.

Guillen is not that. But he's not a saboteur either. There was speculation that he had played Adam Dunn so deep into the 2011 season to publicly embarrass Kenny Williams for such a horrible signing. The longer Dunn played, the conspiracy theory went, the longer Williams would be open to criticism. And the longer Williams was exposed as a poor evaluator of talent, the faster Reinsdorf would choose Ozzie over Kenny. It was silly, uninformed talk.

For all their differences, the two men shared a burning desire to win. Guillen would no more lose a game to make a point than he would sacrifice his firstborn son. And for all the friction between Guillen and Williams, and despite the perception of a broken relationship, the two usually were able to see the bigger picture when decisions needed to be made.

After Oney Guillen tweeted his criticism of the Sox' top draft pick ("another black kid good athlete"), Williams talked with Reinsdorf about Ozzie.

"I told him straight to his face sitting right in the chair

across from his desk, 'I can work with anyone. I don't have any problem working with this man as long as it's a respectful working relationship, and it doesn't get into the personal,'" Williams said.

Even when Guillen and Williams had clashed over Dayan Viciedo during a coaches' meeting earlier in the year, both sides looked on it as a healthy way to do business. There was more than one opinion in the room. In major-league baseball some managers do get a say. Others get what the general manager decides to give them. Guillen and Williams might have been on opposite sides of the Viciedo-Pierre debate, but they were professional enough to move forward for the common good.

"I've never had a problem going in and telling someone right between the eyes what the hell I want to do," Williams said. "You can sit in this position and run it as a dictatorship, but I don't really know anybody smart enough to do that. I prefer to have an all-inclusive style of management that makes allowances for my being talked out of something or being wrong about something.

"I'm not going to say specifically what I wanted to do [with Viciedo] because the fact of the matter is I felt that we could have mixed them in a variety of places because we had enough guys struggling. But that wasn't the overwhelming feeling from my coaching staff. So I chose to acquiesce to their wishes. That's not to be portrayed as an isolated instance. That has happened over the years. Sometimes it works out better than others. Sometimes, I'll stand up and say no, this is going to be the guy. Gavin Floyd, in 2007, I said, 'No, pitch him. He's going to get better. Pitch him.'"

Floyd went 1–5 that season and 17–8 the next.

In early September, Williams and hitting coach Greg Walker got into a shouting match outside the White Sox clubhouse at the Cell. Walker reportedly was upset that Williams had told reporters he liked the swing Gordon Beckham had used at the University of Georgia more than the swing he was bringing to the plate for the Sox.

Williams told Walker to clean out his locker, but cooler heads eventually prevailed, helped along by Reinsdorf, who is a big fan of Walker's. The bright side? For once, it wasn't Guillen and Williams confronting each other.

"Listen, when you're the general manager, we have to explain to him what we think and what we do because he is our boss," Guillen said. "If they get into it with each other, that's their problem. Me and Kenny, we got into it last year not because of baseball but because of something else, and we resolved that problem. We moved on. And I expect the same thing with them."

In 2010, the year Guillen calls his worst in baseball, he and Williams kept their conversations purely professional. Where once they had at least talked with each other about other topics, now they talked about the team and very little else. The Oney affair had put a wall between the two men.

This time, it would be up to Reinsdorf to decide whether the relationship was worth keeping. He had strong feelings for both men. His loyalty to favorite employees is legendary. He is, at times, too loyal, and bad situations in need of resolution tend to fester. It had happened with coach Phil Jackson and general manager Jerry Krause with the Chicago Bulls, whom Reinsdorf also owns. The Jackson-Krause relationship had deteriorated into public pettiness, and Reinsdorf hadn't stepped in to stop it. The difference was that the Bulls were winning NBA titles with all the messiness going on. The White Sox had fought a season-long battle to get above .500 and were in danger of missing the playoffs for the third straight year. Where other owners might have fired Guillen or Williams or both, Reinsdorf had remained fatherly toward both of them.

Somewhere in Williams's job description was the power to fire the manager, even if he and everyone else in Chicago believed that this power resided with Reinsdorf. Reinsdorf might have rolled his eyes at some of the things Guillen said—Reinsdorf referred to him as the Hispanic Jackie Mason—but he enjoyed the manager's personality. It's a personality that couldn't have been more different than his. Reinsdorf doesn't enjoy doing media interviews. When he does, he tries not to say anything controversial.

Guillen made him laugh, always had, and helped keep Reinsdorf young. But Reinsdorf had insisted the year before that Williams would be the one to decide Guillen's fate. There had to be a chain of command, he said, no matter how painful it might be at times.

"The biggest mistake I ever made, but I would make it again, is I let Hawk [general manager Ken Harrelson] fire Tony La Russa [in 1986]," Reinsdorf had told reporters. "I would hope Kenny would never come to that conclusion. But you can't make a general manager have a manager he doesn't want. You can't make a manager have a coach he doesn't want. I can't make the head of the accounting department work with someone he doesn't want. . . . Kenny says he doesn't see it, but that's the way it works."

In an interview with the *Chicago Sun-Times* late in the 2011 season, Williams said that Reinsdorf's description of the chain of command wasn't reality, that the team chairman would have the final say on Guillen's future with the White Sox.

As the season wound down, one of the questions for Reinsdorf & Co. was whether Ozzie was serious about his interest in the Florida job. For more than a year, Guillen's name had been part of the public discussion about the Marlins' managerial situation. It didn't matter whether he brought it up or whether he was simply answering questions about it. It was there.

"If it's time for me to go to the Marlins, I will go with a lot of class," he told Yahoo! Sports in August. "It [would] be an honor to manage the Marlins."

When Guillen backed away from the Marlins at the last second in 2010, Reinsdorf had allowed him to stay with the Sox, even if he might have wondered about his mind-set. But now the same scenario was presenting itself. With Guillen making more noise about being unhappy, had Williams been doing his due diligence with the Marlins in case of another compensation opportunity involving Guillen? And had he indeed been pondering replacements for Guillen? He wasn't saying.

Asked whom he thought Reinsdorf would choose if he had to pick between his manager and general manager, Williams laughed.

"Let me put it to you this way," he said. "I have made it known to Jerry in no uncertain terms that if he can do better than me, that if I am in any way the root cause of our failing to win another World Series in the time in which I thought we would or at least be able to challenge for one, that I am completely okay with him removing me from the position.

And it will be done in a classy, respectful way, and we can go out the next day and have a steak, a cigar, and a glass a wine and have a few laughs.

"That doesn't directly answer your question, other than to give you insight into where I am and how I would not put Jerry in the position to have to choose. If he ultimately thinks there is a choice to be made, it's not because I have pushed that."

It seemed to finally dawn on Guillen that the intrigue over whether he was coming or going could very well blow up in his face. His declarations of devotion to the White Sox became more and more ardent.

"I love this organization," he said. "Love it, love it, love it. See this Sox logo? I'm part of that. I wish I could be in the Hall of Fame one time, so I could wear this freaking uniform. That's how much I love this organization. It's easy when you go to work and you know what you're going to face. The media, the people in the parking lot, the PR department, the fans. I know exactly what the fans behind me are going to say. When you go someplace else, you say, 'Whoop, let me see what we have.' I love the people here, I grew up in this thing."

The same man had sounded a lot different in another column by Joe Cowley in June.

"[Bleep] loyalty," he said. "Like Juan Uribe says, 'Twenty-one million [dollars] is more than twenty million.' "

Three months later, he was singing a different tune, a lovely, soothing lullaby.

"I don't know why people think I'm very tough, very demanding," he said. "I'm a manager who says give me the lineup and play. People have the wrong image of me. What you got? This? Okay, let's go to work. I don't think I have the years to tell the

GM we should do this or that, or the owner. Give me the team, I'll work with the twenty-five guys you give me. It's been like that for a lot of years. I'm not going to sit and say we should have this or that. I'm happy with what I have. It's not my style."

Then why did the whole thing seem to be heading toward White Sox Armageddon? Because this was Ozzie, and the potential for another eruption, for another event is always there.

"Sometimes the same things that propel you to success also can in the end do you in," Williams said as he watched batting practice at the end of August. "Same characteristics, same traits, same drive. It can take you to great heights, and it can bring it all crashing down. That's not just professionally. That's personally, too, if you think about it. The only thing that I can say with certainty is that I am uncertain as to what will happen next."

How about the concept of a boss managing down? That can't be easy for whoever is in charge of Guillen. It won't be easy for Jeffrey Loria in Miami.

"Kenny has to put out fires," John Kruk said in July 2011. "You can understand Kenny's frustration. He's had to put out a lot of fires with Ozzie. But he brought a world championship to that team. They both did. So I think they have that respect for each other. It was interesting talking to them in spring training. I talked to Kenny for a while. I talked to Ozzie for a while. When they speak about each other, I think they're both at a point now where they understand, and they both laugh about it."

Really? They laughed about it? When things were bad, very little about their relationship seemed humorous between the two men.

It took years before Williams finally understood why people seemed so interested in his working relationship with Guillen.

In 2010, the Chicago Blackhawks were on their way to a Stanley Cup title. They had been one of the top teams in the Western Conference the entire season, so when they clinched a playoff spot in late March, it wasn't big news, nor should it have been.

It was why the next day, the *Chicago Sun-Times* didn't seem overly impressed. The news of the playoff berth was not featured on the back page of the newspaper. A photo illustration of Ozzie and Kenny was, pointing the reader to a column inside. The Blackhawks story ran ten pages into the sports section.

Williams saw meaning in that.

"Ozzie and I sell," he said. "A couple weeks later, I asked someone in the organization to explain that to me because I didn't get it. He said, 'At the time, the Hawks hadn't gone any further, and the decision was to put you on the back cover because you guys sell papers.' That told me all I needed to know about how this whole dynamic fits together. The only thing I said was, 'If you can find a good picture, that would be great. If I'm going to be the village idiot, find a good picture, make me look good.' "

What Williams didn't say was what the column was about. He had been asked whether he and Guillen were okay. This was a week after Ozzie had forced Oney to resign after the son's critical tweets.

"We're as okay as we need to be," Williams had said.

As far as encouraging words go, those came with their own wind-chill reading. He could have said everything was fine, that he and Guillen had patched things up. He chose not to.

That was 2010. Now it was 2011, and little had changed. He and Ozzie had been paired together on the back page of the *Sun-Times* several times during the season. None of the stories dealt with a suddenly healthy relationship. Kenny still hated "the peripheral stuff." Ozzie still liked to get his arms around everything.

Lots of people had gotten down to wondering, full-time, what was going to happen to Guillen. FoxSports.com's Ken Rosenthal quoted a source saying that the manager's relationship with Williams "appears unsalvageable," reiterating what Joe Cowley had written a few days before.

The difficulty with pinning down the situation was, of course, Guillen's mercurial personality. He or someone in his circle heard every whisper, meaning his defense system could go to DEFCON 1 in a matter of seconds. One moment, he could be raging about his unresolved future, the next he could be praising Williams.

On the same day Rosenthal reported the alleged untenable working relationship between Williams and Guillen, a kind of diplomacy kicked in. In an interview with the *Sun-Times*, Williams said he had told Reinsdorf, "I can work with anyone, and that includes Ozzie." On the same day Williams was seemingly extending an olive branch, Guillen said he believed Williams should be back for the 2012 season and that fans shouldn't blame the general manager for what happened in 2011.

Somebody had to be wrong, correct? Not necessarily. With Ozzie, things change from second to second. Where he might have been fuming days before about not getting an extension, now he was praising Williams. There was nothing to do but take two Advils and wait for the end of the season, when Reinsdorf would make a decision on the future of both men.

This was life with Ozzie Guillen. It was a spectacle, and it tended to overshadow his team. Where most of what he does as a manager is calculated, it was as if he had no control over himself when it came to the topic of his staying or going.

He was all over the map emotionally. He wanted to remain in Chicago but was braced for no contract extension or for what he considered a low-ball offer from Reinsdorf. And if that happened, leaving would be a matter of self-respect. Then it wouldn't matter if he could get along with Williams or not. He'd be gone.

In the meantime, people were left to wonder whether Ozzie and Kenny could coexist. Reinsdorf wasn't talking publicly.

"I think—I think—there's a mutual respect," Kruk said. "And I think deep down, they like each other somewhere. I couldn't imagine being Ozzie's boss. I couldn't imagine Ozzie saying, 'I need a pitcher. I need a reliever. I need a shortstop. I need a third baseman. Kenny, go get it.'

"I don't know if Ozzie would care about the fact that you can only send a guy down to the minors so many times before he can opt out of his contract or become a free agent or whatever it is. All those little nuances and rules that Kenny has to know in order to get a player, keep a player, send a player down—I'm guessing Ozzie wouldn't care. I can just imagine the patience of Ozzie with a kid that comes up from the minors. A week in the big leagues, you'd better be able to play. If not, we need to get him out."

No, Guillen should never enroll in the Future General Managers of America program. He'd either vow to trade his entire roster or vow to defend it with his life. On the same day. Or maybe in the same sentence.

· 10 ·

IT'S BETTER TO BE THE MATADOR THAN THE BULL (USUALLY)

The Chicago White Sox were long gone in the American League Central race. It was late September 2011, and a reconnaissance plane wouldn't have helped them find the Detroit Tigers. There was nothing to do but wait for the season to be put out of its misery.

Ozzie Guillen hunched forward in the Sox dugout before a game against the Kansas City Royals and considered the subject of gore. No, not Adam Dunn's season. Bullfighting, his passion.

"Managers have time to think. Bullfighters don't," he said. "They've got to react. They know one little bad move—you put the cape on the wrong side—you're dead or you're going to get hurt. When the bullfighters kill the bull, they're so close to the horn, they can get killed instantly, just like the bull can. People don't know that. Sometimes the horn is right on the chest or the side. You can get killed if you make a mistake or you're asleep. If you're asleep in the dugout, it's an out. You fall asleep out in the bullfighting ring, you have a chance to be a dead man."

All managers have shelf lives. The happy, energized manager who puts on a baseball cap and smiles for the cameras at his introductory press conference will look run-down and beaten up when he gets fired years later. The owner holds the door for him as he leaves.

The bull tells the bullfighter when it's time to move on, even if the matador doesn't always listen.

"Right now, one of my best bullfighter friends, he wants to do a retirement bullfight," Guillen said. "I said, 'Why do you want to do this? You're crazy. You're going to get killed.' He said, 'If I get killed in the ring, I don't care.' I said, 'You've got a better chance of getting killed than you do of killing the bull because you're old and out of shape.' In baseball when you retire, you hit a grounder to the shortstop, you take your hat off and say, 'Thank you.' In bullfighting, it's easy to get killed. If your reaction time is gone, it's over. That's when you know it's time to retire."

It's trickier with a manager, though a lot less bloody. The smart ones know from the beginning that they've been hired to be fired. The ones who don't are deluding themselves. The lucky ones get to walk away of their own volition.

What tells a manager when it's time to retire?

"When the players don't want to play for him anymore," Guillen said. "I will call my shot. I know when it's time to go. I've spent so much time in baseball and I love baseball so much, but sometimes I think, 'Do I really like this shit?' "

What came next as he sat in the Sox dugout was classic, uncut Ozzie. He went on a screed about money that lasted a few minutes and had him pacing in the dugout by the time it was over. He was finished with the Sox, even though he wasn't verbalizing it. That same day, unbeknownst to the public, he had met with Reinsdorf and officially asked for a contract extension. Reinsdorf had officially said no. Ozzie could manage the final year of his contract in 2012, the chairman said, and they could see where they stood after that.

It's why, hours later, the subject of bullfighting had suddenly given way to the subject of money.

"I'm good at what I do, and I do it with passion," Guillen said. "I do it with love. I do it with commitment. I don't do it because I want to kiss somebody's ass. In the past I did it because of money. Yes.

"Everybody told me to play for the love of the game. Fuck them. That's lying shit. People play the game because of fucking money. It's the only thing we can do. If we can make more money somewhere else, that's how it is. I hate when players say, 'Oh, I'll play for the love of the game.' Fine. There are a lot of softball games out there. Just go play for a softball team.

"They say, 'Oh, I only play for fun.' No you don't. You play because you're getting paid a lot of money. If I say that, people get mad at me, but it's a bunch of shit. You're not going to travel for three hours in a plane, pack and unpack, and not see your kid for twenty straight days, not see your kid grow up. You play for the love of the game? You're full of shit."

Guillen's problems with the White Sox had little to do with money, but money was a convenient outlet for his anger at Kenny Williams and whoever and whatever else he believed had brought him to this turning point in his life.

"People say, 'Oh, I want a championship ring,'" he said. "No, motherfucker, you play to be rich, and then you win a goddamn ring. Fuck that shit. Everybody after they make a bunch of money wants to play for a winning team. People play baseball and other sports to be rich. People don't play for fucking rings.

"With a ring, you're not going to send a kid to college. You're not going to take care of your grandkids. You're not going to have the house you want. You'll be another piece of shit. You can have ten rings on your fingers and if you're fucking poor, you're not shit. The only thing you have is people hug you and say, 'Hey, great job. You're the best. Thank you.' Yeah, motherfucker, but I'm starving here."

This was Guillen's way of cutting his emotional ties with the Sox, even if he wasn't saying it directly. Over the previous few years, his relationship with Williams had eroded into mostly behind-the-scenes pettiness that occasionally flared in public. Guillen's side hated what it perceived as Williams's pompousness. Williams's backers rolled their eyes at what they perceived as Ozzie's constant need for attention.

So it became about money, even if it wasn't about money. Money was the metaphor for the respect Guillen felt the Sox weren't giving him. For all his talk about taking the blame for what had transpired in a disappointing season, he believed he had worked as hard as he ever had—had, in fact, managed his ass off.

Now he talked and paced, full of energy and frustration. Every once in a while, he'd look up toward the suites where the White Sox brass sat during games.

"With the rings, I can't do shit with that," he said. "But with money, I can go buy me a new boat, I can go buy me a new car, I can dress my wife the way I want to dress her, I can go to Spain. With the ring, I can go to United Airlines and say, 'Hello, I won the 2005 championship. Can you fly me to Spain?' Hell, fuck no.

"Money is everything besides health. Money is next to that. A lot of people say, 'Oh, love.' They don't know what love means. I guarantee you, if you raise a girl where I grew up and you've got no money and she loves you, but you put the same girl with a guy who's got a lot of money, I'll bet she'll love the guy with money. That's the way it is. I love you, but I'm hungry.

"I work in this job for fucking money. I don't work for nothing. Money. That's it. The ring? Fuck the ring. I don't even wear my fucking rings. I don't."

Did he mention he wanted a boat?

"You know what I saw a couple days ago?" he said. "I saw a fucking sixty-two-foot boat—two million dollars. That's what I want, and that's what I'm going to get. People have to pay me for that. White Sox? I don't know. Marlins? I don't know. But somebody will pay. I want to buy my fucking boat. That's my inspiration. My inspiration is money. That's everybody's inspiration.

"If I leave here, I will say, 'I leave here because I want to make my fucking money. You know why? Because no fucking fans, no fucking Jerry or fucking anybody is going to take care of my grandkids and put me in a sixty-two-foot boat.' That's why there's free agency."

The thing about free agency is that it takes willing partners. There had been no indications the Cubs were interested in Ozzie, and in a perfect-world scenario (other than Kenny Williams's banishment to a former Soviet-bloc republic) a job on the North Side of Chicago would have been very appealing. It would have allowed him to stay in Chicago. But Guillen didn't have time to wait for the Cubs, who would eventually hire Milwaukee Brewers hitting coach Dale Sveum as manager, to come to their senses. The Marlins were at his figurative doorstep.

The early reports suggested that they were willing to give him a four-year contract worth $16 million. The reports were wrong. He would take the job for $10 million over four years. The average of $2.5 million per year was about the same amount he would have made in Chicago had he stayed for the 2012 season.

It wasn't about money or a boat. To some extent, it was about security. If he had remained with the Sox, he didn't know what the future would hold beyond 2012. He didn't know what managerial jobs would be open, and he understood that there might not be as eager a suitor as the Marlins.

But it was also about knowing that the fight was over and that he had lost. No contract extension meant that Williams had won. Ozzie couldn't take another year of squabbles and uncertainty.

Three days later, the announcement would come down that he was going to the Marlins.

And those words from way back in spring training, the ones from Ozzie that promised no drama in the 2011 season? What happened to them? They had sped away, like a boat caught in the Gulf Stream.

Was Guillen's ending in Chicago an anomaly, or does it always have to end messy for him?

Messy is the best guess.

Earlier in the season, Guillen seemed to acknowledge the challenges of having him as a manager.

"I cannot picture myself managing another ball club," he

said. "I don't think other teams are going to put up with my shit."

When the Sox decided they didn't want Guillen back as a player after the 1997 season, he went out with a bang, ripping the front office.

"They're all fake," he told the *Chicago Tribune* at the time, after signing as a free agent with the Baltimore Orioles. "I deserved better—not because I had been there a long time, but because I did a lot for them. It was my fault. I did all those things when maybe I shouldn't have. . . . They talk about being fan-friendly, media-friendly. That's what I am. They give Albert [Belle] all that money, and he doesn't do anything for them. They won't give me $500,000, and that's my organization."

Despite those poison-tipped words, Jerry Reinsdorf would be the one to suggest to Williams that he at least interview Guillen for the Sox managerial job in late 2003.

And Reinsdorf would be the one who let Guillen out of the final year of his contract so that he could manage the Marlins, despite the high probability Guillen would leave scorched earth behind.

That's the way it is with Ozzie, and it's why the Sox were braced for anything as he walked into the interview room at the Cell following his last game as manager. For the record, the White Sox beat the Toronto Blue Jays 4–3 on September 26, 2011, to end his career in Chicago.

"All the people out there that hate me, now they're happy," he said, smiling. "And other people like me."

Guillen did not bring a flamethrower with him to his final press conference. He was gracious and generous.

"If anybody in Chicago is going to blame Kenny or Jerry or the front-office people, they're wrong," he said.

Who would ever do that, Ozzie?

He said he didn't know what the future held for him, though a few hours later his website would run a post stating how excited he was about joining the Marlins. Oops. The premature announcement was quickly taken down. Williams would later say he was glad no reporter had asked him after Ozzie's last game about the possibility that the Marlins and Guillen had had earlier, improper conversations.

Maybe that's how it was meant to end, tangled and sloppy, with a dash of chaos thrown in.

The Marlins would later agree to send two minor leaguers, reliever Jhan Marinez and infielder Osvaldo Martinez—an Ozzie-for-Ozzie trade!—to the Sox as compensation.

Guillen said all the right things: that he hadn't earned a contract extension, not with the team's eventual third-place finish and 79–83 record; that he admired Reinsdorf for thinking with his brain and not his heart; and that if he had stayed, he would have been able to work with Williams.

But doubt did seep in when he thanked the Sox for letting him walk and pursue "what is best for me."

"Maybe it's not the best, maybe it's the worst," he said. "I don't know what's out there. Maybe I'm dreaming or I might not appreciate what I got here. You don't know. It's just something that you have to [turn] the page and move on. That's life. Hopefully the next book treat me the same way this book treat me."

If you were going to write a treatise on how to bow out gracefully from a management job, you would do well to study how Guillen did it that night. He did not shoot even one arrow. He did not rip Williams, Williams's restaurant, Williams's offspring, or anything associated with the general manager. He called his departure a "both-sides situation."

For his part, Williams expressed bewilderment that the Ozzie Era had ended in a two-car crash.

"I wish I had a dollar for every time I had that thought, Why did it have to come to this?" he said. "I don't have answers."

This being Ozzie, it didn't mean he was done talking or that his people were done talking. It didn't mean that at all. He always reserves the right to say more. He has a standing reservation to say more.

For Guillen, part of the fun of managing is standing on the front step of the dugout during games and interacting with fans. Like a hyperactive kid, he is easily distracted. He converses with the people sitting nearby. He talks trash. He looks at the pretty girls. He makes jokes that make the fans laugh.

For eight years, he had done that in Chicago, and now he was leaving. He had read enough e-mails, letters, and tweets to know that there were loads of people who liked him and loads who didn't. There was very little in between. Either way, it took energy and effort to handle him. Miami will find this out eventually.

"I know [Sox fans] are not going to forget me," he declared at his farewell in Chicago. "They can't. Even if they want to, they can't. They walk to the ballpark, my picture is going to be up there. I hope they don't take it down."

Guillen admitted in his introductory press conference in Miami that he had been "dragging myself to the clubhouse" the final two years with the White Sox. It was time to go.

"The whole thing here kind of ran its course," said Paul Konerko. "It got to a point where it got so stressful. Something had to give. I don't think he ever wanted to leave here, but I think both sides are probably going to be relieved and happy."

Jim Bowden, the former general manager of the Cincinnati Reds and the Washington Nationals, saw something darker ahead.

"In Miami, Guillen's colorful personality certainly will sell tickets and bring some much-needed levity to a losing situation," Bowden wrote on ESPN.com. "In the short term, that works for the Marlins. But when the honeymoon is over in the dog days of August, when color and personality turn to vitriol and venom, will the Marlins think Guillen was worth it? Somehow I doubt it."

The Marlins' payroll was expected to jump from $58 million in 2011 to $95 million-plus in 2012. It's not the $127 million payroll the White Sox had in 2011, but how did that work out anyway?

When the Marlins introduced Guillen as their new manager on September 28, the doubts that had cropped up in his Chicago farewell were gone. He was excited that Miami seemed serious about investing in players. He had taken a tour of the new stadium and was thoroughly impressed. There's nothing like a $515 million ballpark with a retractable roof to make a man think he has made the right decision.

Jeffrey Loria said he wasn't worried a bit about his manager's famous outspokenness.

"I couldn't care less about [ruffled] feathers," he said. "I don't have any feathers. And I don't care about him ruffling anybody. Ozzie has his opinions, and he's entitled to them. You know that going in. But Ozzie comes with a great pedigree."

If that truly is Loria's attitude, then their relationship has a good chance of running smoothly. It takes an owner who sees the bigger picture to fully understand Guillen. With

Ozzie, there will always be fires that require extinguishing. But some of those fires end up helping the team.

Loria hired Guillen to turn around a moribund franchise, but he also hired him to help bring fans to the new park. Part of Guillen's public appeal is his habit of saying anything at any time. To turn around and tell him he needs to learn discretion would be counterproductive, not to mention futile.

Loria called Guillen a "category-five manager," a hurricane of a man, a force of nature. He meant it as a positive, but surely he knows that description could come back to haunt him if Guillen leaves behind a wide path of destruction.

Five days after saying "fuck the rings," Ozzie reworked his thoughts about money for the Miami media.

"My biggest satisfaction in this game is rings," he said. "My goal is to have more money."

A short time later, Guillen and his family boarded a plane for a sixteen-day vacation in Spain. It was time to watch some bullfighting. When he returned, ESPN announced that he would be part of the *Baseball Tonight* show during the World Series, reuniting him with John Kruk, his former minor-league teammate. The network would keep one eye on the ratings and one finger on the bleep button.

Ozzie was saying one thing publicly and quite another thing privately. When Williams named Don Cooper the interim manager for the last two games of the season, Guillen sent his pitching coach a searing text: "You finally got what you wanted."

Guillen was upset that Cooper had gone to Williams to ask for a contract extension. Guillen said the meeting had taken place behind his back in June. Cooper said the meeting occurred in early August and that there was nothing underhanded about it. He said he had informed Ozzie and the other coaches of his intentions. After twenty-four years in the Sox organization, he said, he had earned the right to talk to the general manager about his future as the team's pitching coach, rather than wait for Guillen to speak for all the coaches.

Williams gave Cooper a four-year extension. Guillen struck out swinging on his own contract extension. This was especially upsetting to Ozzie, who had always fought hard for his coaches come contract time. He believes most major-league coaches are woefully underpaid.

"If you fire a coach from here, there's a line from here to fucking Chicago to want to coach in the big leagues," he had said in spring training. "Coaching in the big leagues is not a good job. The coaches in fucking high school make more money than coaches in the big leagues. Maybe you got two, three guys making pretty good money. Everybody else's pay sucks.

"You put all the coaches together for an average salary, it's fucking terrible. In the NBA, how many players do you have? Twelve. How many fucking coaches do they have? Twenty. You only have to worry about two, three players. I got one hitting coach and one pitching coach. And when they fuck it up, people want us to get fired."

Brent Lillibridge and minor leaguer Lastings Milledge were two unproven players who made more money than Cooper or Greg Walker, Guillen said. And it bothered him.

"Who's got more responsibility?" he said. "They don't say Milledge and Lillibridge are fucking horseshit. It's 'Greg Walker can't teach them how to hit.' Those players make $400,000. Walker makes maybe $100,000. Who takes more heat? Who spends more time on the fucking field? Greg Walker worries about twelve guys. Milledge and Lillibridge worry about themselves, and they make half a million dollars a year.

"Look at fucking college baseball coaches. Those guys don't know shit about the game. They don't know nothing about baseball. They know, 'This is the way we play. This is the way the program is. We hit like this. We're going to catch the ball like this. We're going to throw like that. We're going to run the bases like this.' They don't know fucking shit about baseball.

"They make a lot of fucking money. They make more money than all my coaches. I don't know why coaches in the big leagues get treated like that."

But Cooper getting an extension and a two-game stint as interim manager? It was too much for Guillen and some of the other coaches, who operated in a world of gossip and suspicion.

Williams made a vague threat about legal action against Joe Cowley of the *Chicago Sun-Times*, who had written that Cooper had been reporting to the general manager what Guillen and the coaches had been saying in private—in other words, that Cooper was a spy in his general manager's service. Cooper vehemently denied the report. The other side thought Joey Cora was an agitator who got Guillen worked up regularly and needlessly.

For all of Ozzie's assertions that he always pushed for better pay for his coaches, Cooper said it wasn't true.

"I was told that Ozzie was asked, 'What about your coaches? Let's sign your coaches,'" Cooper told radio station WSCR in Chicago. "And he said, 'No, let them sweat.'"

All the small, nasty things that had been volleyed back and forth behind the scenes were now on full display. The best face the Sox had put on now was impossible to look at without grimacing. Again.

When Guillen returned from his vacation, Cowley contacted him and told him what Cooper had said on the radio. That led to another public explosion from Guillen, complete with accusations that Cooper had sold his soul to Williams.

"Cooper needs to look in the mirror," Guillen told the *Sun-Times*. "He didn't backstab me. I know who he is. He backstabbed his fellow coaches, the guys he worked with for years. You got family? That's fine. Everyone does. We all knew Coop was Kenny's bitch.

"Look, Coop is not a good coach. He's a great coach. But Coop is Coop. He doesn't worry about anyone, he worries about himself. I stuck up for my coaches.

"I told [the Sox] I want to keep my coaching staff, and I never lied to the media. I talked to Jerry Reinsdorf maybe five times [about extending the coaches' contracts over the years]. The reason I was so comfortable with the Sox was the coaches. Let them sweat it out? Coop was Kenny's guy, and my staff knew that. We all know what he really is."

And just for good measure, Ozzie took one more shot at the White Sox. It likely wasn't his last one.

"Since last year, this was about integrity, it was about loyalty, it was about do they want me here," he said. "Let me say it my way. The Sox were saying, 'Yes, we want to [bleep] you, but we don't want to marry you.'"

Are you sure you're ready for Ozzie, Miami?

One of the problems with the 2011 White Sox was that there wasn't a prick in the bunch. Brent Morel was quiet. Brent Lillibridge was nice. Adam Dunn rarely turned down a media request and was almost always polite, even as he was asked to walk through the slop of his slump again and again.

The only person liable to get testy was Carlos Quentin, and that was only if someone attempted to pierce the shield he had erected to keep reporters away. Jake Peavy was volatile on the mound, but a good old boy off it. Plus, he was a newcomer and a pitcher, which meant he lacked the weight that a longtime White Sox or an everyday player carried in the clubhouse.

So it was always up to Ozzie to shake things up, not that he ever resented it. That's just the way it was.

"I wish all my players hate me and we win," he said. "That would be awesome. I don't like having friends and being in last place. They hate me, and we win a championship? Please do. I don't like them being friends, eating at my house, and sending me Christmas cards, and my butt is on the line every time."

Guillen doesn't want anyone to hate him. You can count on that. But it will happen wherever he goes. One person's entertaining manager is another's loudmouth. He's polarizing without even trying.

A few other givens as Ozzie rolls forward.

—When the Marlins are struggling, he'll talk, often, about getting fired.

—He and Loria will have their share of dustups, especially if the owner acts out during games.

—A person or group will feel insulted by something Guillen says. The mayor of Miami. Marine biologists. Cuban Americans. Somebody.

—He won't spend too much time worrying about it.

"I'm only scared of one thing in my life: die without seeing my grandchild grow up," he said. "Everything else, I'm not scared. Nothing. One thing about it, my short life will be very long. I had fun in this game. I do everything in this game. I had fun everywhere. I do everything I want to do. That's why I say, the day I'm gonna die, I'll be happy."

It's hard to picture a world without Ozzie Guillen. There would be a large hole where he used to stand. There would be stillness where sound waves used to vibrate.

He has talked about the perfect way to exit the planet.

"I hope I die on the field," he said in a 2009 *Chicago Tribune* interview. "I hope when I walk to change the pitcher, I drop dead and that's it. I know my family would be so happy that it happened on the field. They wouldn't feel bad because that's what I've always wanted to do."

Two years later, at the end of a frustrating season, he talked about the end, baseball-wise. As he did, he let out all the frustration and the pain of leaving the White Sox and beginning fresh somewhere else. It wasn't cathartic. It was Ozzie.

"If I win one more fucking title, I might not ever come back to this game. There's a good chance," he said. "This game is a lot of politics, a lot of hypocritical people, a lot of bullshit, a lot of kiss ass, and I'm not any of those things."

No, he's not. Not even close.

• AFTERWORD •

EXPAND THE BRAND

Spring Training, 2012

On a warm, sunny day in Jupiter, Florida, pitchers and catchers with smiles on their faces are standing on a field at the Miami Marlins' spring-training facility. It's the best time of year, late February, not just because the weather is near perfect but because life is near perfect. Baseball is shaking itself out of hibernation. The pain, frustration, and bone-weariness of the previous season are gone. For the Marlins, it's as if a blessed, teamwide amnesia has settled in.

They have bought a boatload of talent to fill the beautiful new ballpark that sits waiting for them in the Little Havana section of Miami—including Jose Reyes, the All-Star shortstop and National League batting champion; Heath Bell, one of the game's top closers; Mark Buehrle, the veteran White Sox starter; and Carlos Zambrano, the still-fearsome Cubs pitcher who had worn out his welcome in Chicago. They have signed Ozzie Guillen to caffeinate a sleepy organization. Hope springs eternal for all major-league teams in February, but it has a noticeable skip in its step this year in Jupiter.

And here stands Guillen in the middle of it all, giving the players a taste of what to expect from him. He has traded his White Sox uniform for a Marlins uniform—white pants and a black jersey with what is meant to be a festive multicolored MIAMI splashed across the front. A week before, he had said the uniforms "look bad." Of course he had. People were expecting tact?

Now Ozzie is introducing the minor-league coaches and trainers, and as he speaks you can almost see the same thought bubble above the heads of the players: What, exactly, is *this*?

"If you have trouble with any of these fucking people," Guillen says, pointing to the staff, "you're going to have a problem with me. I don't think that's funny. I'm very easy. I love to have fun. I'll fuck around with you guys, but I like this shit the right way. How? We're going to practice the right way, and we're going to do the stuff the right way. If we come in and we fuck around, we're going to stay a little longer. And don't worry, I can stay here all day. My wife's in town. Fuck, I don't want to see her."

That last bit is pure Ozzie, part tension-defuser, part take-my-wife-please Henny Youngman. The players laugh. Their shoulders noticeably relax.

He talks about the importance of being ready. Be ready for a great year, he says. Be ready to get where you want to go, he says. The players can work with this. This is spring-training comfort food. They have heard this from every manager they've ever had. They can chew on being ready, they can digest it. Then Guillen moves on to the subject of tardiness. In its most narrow interpretation, the rule is to not be late at all, but . . .

"If you're late, make sure you call somebody," Ozzie begins. "Give me a good excuse. Just tell me the truth: 'I'm late because I went with a guy or chick last night. We fell asleep and we couldn't wake up.' Just make sure you tell me the truth. You lie to me and I find out, we've got a problem. If you're drunk and you can't go out on the field, you tell me. I'll send you to the trainer's room, and we'll take care of that."

It's clear that the players aren't exactly sure what to make of Ozzie. They have heard things about him, seen him on ESPN in mid-tirade against an umpire, or watched him do playoff analysis for one of the networks. But until you've experienced him firsthand, until you've marinated in his spices, you can't fully understand his approach.

"I love to have fun in the game because when I was a player, the only thing I did was have fun," he tells them. "I expect everyone here to have fun. How do you have fun? Win fucking games."

He and many of the people standing in front of him know this to be true. He had just gone through a painful season in 2011, as had some of the pitchers and catchers standing before him. In this way, they are kindred spirits desperately looking for the same thing: the erasure of last season from their memories.

Later, after the players had dispersed, Guillen explained his speech-making methodology. It has to do with making sure players know what he's all about. Immediately.

"The message most of the time is the same message with every manager," he said. "But in the meanwhile, you come down here, a lot of kids twenty-two, twenty-three years old, they might be wondering who this guy really is. I will show them who I am and how they're going to play for me. . . . Have some fun. I just told a couple people, if they love me in September the way they love me right now, we're in good shape."

Bell, the closer who came to the Marlins from the San Diego Padres, seems to grasp Guillen the best. Then again, he's the man who a few minutes earlier had been walking around the clubhouse bare-chested, with his pants hitched up to his chest and a mask over his face like a professional wrestler. He likes to see his teammates relaxed. He already has vowed to give the moody Carlos Zambrano a hug every day he sees a smile on the right-hander's face. Longtime observers of Zambrano predict Bell's 2012 hugging average will be well below the Mendoza Line.

But Bell's description of having the proper mental approach to the game sounds right out of Ozzie's School of Management: Get Rid of the Clutter in Their Heads.

"When you're having fun, you're relaxed, you're loose, and you can just go perform," says Bell, an All-Star the previous three seasons. "If you're all uptight, like my pants are right now, it's really hard to go out there and perform. If you think you're going to lose your job, if you think you have to get that out, you have to get a hit, you're not going to go out there and let your ability play. So if you can go out there and ease up and relax and let your ability come out, then you're going to perform and do great things."

Guillen already is setting a tone of looseness, but he knows it has its limits.

"If you're having fun and you're losing, you look like an idiot," he says.

Some of the players might have walked away a bit bewildered by Guillen's address, but the message, wrapped in his distinctive language, is to play hard, always. That's it. Don't ever give less than your all, because then you'll be on Ozzie's shit list.

And if you have a problem with the manager, tell him about it. Same as it ever was with Ozzie.

"It's refreshing to see," says Marlins outfielder Logan Morrison, an avid user of Twitter who is Guillen's equal when it comes to social-media unpredictability. "Ozzie has a free spirit, and he makes no issues about who he is. He doesn't try to hide anything. I feel like that's kind of what my personality is. If he has a problem with you, he's going to let you know. It's kind of the way I am. If I have a problem with you, I'm going to let you know. It's not anything that I have to adapt to. Maybe guys don't like it. But what I've seen so far, I've liked it."

The day before, Guillen had met with the front-office staff. When Marlins president of baseball operations Larry Beinfest was asked whether there was anything about Ozzie that had stood out, he laughed.

"All of the twenty-minute meeting we just had," he said.

The theme of the meeting was that the Marlins' last-place finish in 2011 was being moved from the "True Crime" section of the library to "Ancient History." It was over with, done. But in addition to that, Guillen wanted the people in the building to know that whatever impression they had of him likely was wrong.

"I had butterflies because you're going to talk to people you don't know," he said later. "People have to know who you really are. A lot of people think they know: 'Fuck, I'm going to play for this guy. Oh, my God.' They only see me on TV.

"But when you see me every day, I'm very different from

what people think about me. That's why I have to let them know I'm not going to put up with any crap. I don't. I don't care who you are. I don't care how much money you make. That's the way it is.

"But in the meanwhile, don't walk around me like I kill people or eat [live] chickens. No, I'm a very fun, open guy, but my leash is pretty short. We've got to do the right thing, starting with my coaches."

Neither that meeting with the front-office staff nor the talk with the pitchers and catchers was the Speech, the one he would give to the entire team when the position players showed up at camp.

"That's the tape meeting," he says. "Put a recorder there, and you'll never forget that motherfucker. You'll say to your grandchild, 'You want to see something funny? Here he is.' Bring earplugs, because I will tell the players the way it is. Maybe they never hear that thing before. Maybe a couple guys. Mark Buehrle did. He'll be laughing. But everybody else will be like, 'Oh, what's going on here?' But that's who I am.

"I'm going to have the owner there. Everyone. Because when the thing is going down, it's going to be Ozzie's fault. When we win the fucking championship, [people will say,] 'Thank God [Jeffrey] Loria and Beinfest put all those players together. They spent a lot of money. Look how good we are.' But as soon as the shit goes down, they'll say, 'It's your fault.' And I will take it."

By now, the veteran Ozzie watcher will know what's coming. It might be the first day of spring training in Guillen's first year as the manager of the Miami Marlins, but it's never too early to start deflecting unwanted attention from the players. It's never too early to let everyone know that your shoulders were made to bear a heavy load. It's never too early to Protect Your Employees from the Barbarians.

And that other f-word—*fired*—well, February of your first season is as good a time as any to bring it up.

"Believe me, if the Marlins go now and hit .210, all of a sudden it'll be Ozzie's fault," Guillen says. "I'll take it. That's fine. I'm not afraid of that. I'm not afraid to get fired. I'm not. I will find a job. I'm not afraid.

"If we lose, I will take the blame because I'm strong enough to do that and tough enough to do that. Just go out and play. [The Marlins] spent a lot of time and a lot of money and a lot of belief. They spent all the time and the money and they believed I was the guy to run this ball club. I feel proud, but there's a lot of weight on your shoulders. I don't worry about 'fail.' I'd rather fail with a ball club like that and know I have a chance to win every day than, as soon as I go to the ballpark, I say, 'Oh, I know I'm going to get fired today because we don't have the team.'

"But you give me the team and we fail, I'll be the first one to say, bro, I never run from negative. I never run from being criticized. I sometimes get upset when people say something I never said or people take advantage of who I am. If we don't play the right way, I will take the blame. My players are going to play the right way. I don't care how we're going to do it, but we have twenty-five guys and we're going to pull the same rope. If we have one or two guys that don't want to pull the same rope, then we'll see what we can do."

This is Ozzie in his natural state, braced for a moment of impact that hasn't yet presented itself. But that isn't the point, of course. This is a declaration, a letter of intent. He will absorb any unwanted attention aimed at his players so that they can concentrate on baseball. And if Guillen happens to be wired in a way that allows him to actually enjoy the attention and the abuse, what of it? If it helps his team win games, let him be a happy, yapping punching bag.

Hanley Ramirez walked into the Marlins' spring-training clubhouse wearing gym shoes that were black, aqua, and something between pink and coral.

"He's got the most amazing shoes I've ever seen," Guillen said. "I said, 'To wear those shoes, you better hit forty home runs. You wear those shoes and you hit like Ozzie, that's not a good-looking shoe.' That shows you how good he is. You are who you are. You do what you're supposed to do, those shoes are going to look very good on you."

Ozzie could be the perfect manager or the worst nightmare for the temperamental Ramirez. It will depend on whether Ramirez plays hard all the time. If he does, Guillen will protect him with a Secret Service agent's tenacity. If Ramirez hustles, Guillen will stand up for him the way he did for Adam Dunn in Chicago. If he doesn't, Guillen will bench him the way he benched Alex Rios.

The first order of business was to take Ramirez's temperature over being moved from shortstop to third base to make room for Reyes, the former New York Mets shortstop who was the Marlins' big off-season signing. Besides being a huge talent, Ramirez has a reputation for self-centeredness. How would he react to being relocated?

"I don't worry about Hanley," Guillen said. "We talked. I'm the type of guy, I'm not going to lie to anybody like, 'Yeah, I talked to Hanley and everything was great' when it's not. We talked, and he wasn't happy. Of course you can't be happy. But I said, 'Let spring training start, when you see all these people around you, the attitude of the ball club, the talent you have. Let me tell you what the goal is.' He'll be fine. I think we did a good job to stay away from him the last couple weeks.

"Let Hanley be Hanley. There's one thing about him that's my concern: he will play the way everybody should be playing. That's my goal. He's going to be mad, he's going to be upset, he's going to be sad, he's going to be happy. That's his problem. Our problem is just everyone in general, twenty-five players.

"I'll say it again: they built this ball club around him. He might not know it, but we did. We want to make him better, and we want to win. I think he's a big part of this ball club."

Ramirez battled injuries in 2011, hitting just .243, a career low by almost fifty points. When he's healthy and happy, he can be great. He has won a batting crown (.342 in 2009, a year in which he also had 106 runs batted in), led the league in runs scored (125 in 2008), and twice stolen more than fifty bases in a season.

Whenever Ramirez faced the Mets and Reyes, his Dominican Republic countryman, the competition seemed to bring out the best in him. The Marlins were hoping that, now that they were playing side by side, the pair would inspire each other on a daily basis. Ozzie looked like the perfect person to keep things running smoothly between these two proud and talented men.

"He's a good guy," Ramirez said of Guillen. "You've just got to show him that you come to play every day and hustle. That's what he likes his players to do. That's all. . . . You can go 0-for-4, but if he sees you giving everything you've got, he's going to be cool with it."

How can Ozzie nourish all the needy personalities on the Marlins? He can't. The players will have to do most of the motivating themselves. Reyes can be one of the best players in baseball when he wants to be. He wanted to be in 2011, a contract year, when he led the National League with a .337 average. In return, Miami gave him a six-year, $106 million contract. But 2012? That was the question, a huge question. The Marlins were praying that all the newness they had been marketing—particularly the new manager—would inspire Reyes.

"Ozzie is special," said Jeffrey Loria, the team owner. "He is a magnetic draw with players."

All of Guillen's considerable managerial skills will be called to active duty to handle Zambrano, who had enough emotional explosions with the Chicago Cubs that he almost made Ozzie look like the pacifist in town. Almost. In 2007, Zambrano punched out his catcher, Michael Barrett. In 2010, after giving up four runs in the first inning of a game against the White Sox, he had to be separated from his teammate Derrek Lee during a dugout meltdown. In August 2011, the Cubs suspended him for the remainder of the season after he twice threw at the Atlanta Braves' Chipper Jones, got kicked out of the game, cleared out his locker, and reportedly told trainers and clubhouse staff that he was retiring.

In the off-season the Cubs gave up, trading him and cash to the Marlins for pitcher Chris Volstad.

Guillen doesn't dispute that Zambrano, a fellow Venezuelan, has had anger issues, but he wonders whether others dropped the ball. Perhaps someone in a position of authority with the Cubs should have learned to see the warning signs, to notice the lit fuse sizzling toward the dynamite, he said.

"Maybe it's not his fault," Guillen said. "Maybe it's somebody's fault. Maybe they let that tiger leave the cage and couldn't bring him back. That tiger is not going to leave the cage. I guarantee you he is not leaving the cage. I guarantee you that. As soon as he tries to open the cage, I'll be waiting for his ass.

"I never had any problem about players going all crazy. No, I didn't. We never had problems in the clubhouse. I throw a lot of people under the bus, [but] we never had any problems. They know why. I don't see any problem with Carlos.

"Do I want him to get pissed? Of course I do. But take it easy, tiger. Like I say, in Venezuela, there's the bull and the goddamned matador. He will be dead in two seconds because I know how to kill the bull at the right time."

It's worth noting that after the confrontation with Lee in 2010, which led to a suspension and anger-management counseling for the volatile pitcher, Zambrano dined that night with Ozzie. It raises the question of whether a manager and player should be friends.

"Off the field, he's my friend, but I have to respect him," Zambrano said. "I have a mission here that I have to treat him in the clubhouse as a professional and as a manager. I have a lot of respect for him. I'm happy to play for Ozzie. I'm happy to be one of his twenty-five men on the roster."

Guillen doesn't foresee problems.

"People have a pool in Venezuela to see what day we're going to fight," he said, laughing. "I'm not going to fight with him. I don't want to get my butt kicked. But I will fight. If Carlos gets mad at the umpire or gets mad at himself, that's fine. But don't get involved with your teammates. And don't be throwing at people when you don't have to do it. I guarantee that ain't going to happen. I guarantee it."

Can anyone guarantee anything with Zambrano?

"Is Carlos going to throw at somebody without my permission, with no reason?" Guillen went on. "I don't think it's going to happen. He might have a reason. Well, go ahead."

Near the end of the first spring-training workout, Zambrano threw a faux brushback pitch at Ozzie, who had been leaning on a bat near home plate.

"That's the last time he throws at somebody," Guillen said, smiling. He's confident he can be the one manager who harnesses the good in Zambrano, the manager who finds the perfect middle ground between the pitcher's passionate competitiveness and his dark, angry side.

"If there's anybody to fix him or keep him on the right track, I think it would be Ozzie," said Buehrle. "But that's between those two."

There was a lot of laughter in the clubhouse during the opening of camp, but everyone understood what was at stake. The Marlins spent more money than they'd ever spent and asked Guillen to manage a team full of personalities, ranging from wacky (Bell) to flammable (Zambrano). They asked him to bring his gut instincts to the dugout and adapt them for the National League.

There will be a big audience watching, not just in Miami, but wherever people enjoy baseball. The Marlins and Guillen were scheduled to be the subject of Showtime's reality series *The Franchise* in 2012. Viewers will see an excitable manager who has a lot on his mind. And whatever is on his mind will find its way to the nearest microphone.

Besides having much to say, Guillen has much to prove.

"I just got fired," he said, ignoring the fact that he was allowed to walk away from the White Sox. "I have to prove to people how good I am. Every year. If you had a bad year, you have to prove you're better than that. If you have a great year, you have to prove, 'I'm that good.' Every year, you've got to prove to people how good you can be. That's a good thing.

"My point is, change your attitude. This is not the [old] Marlins: 'Okay, let's go play, there are two people in the stands, no media coverage.' It's a different thing now. It's a different scenario. Show you're ready to handle it every day.

"I will take care of the media and the fans. They're all mine. Hate me. Don't hate my players. I'll take care of that. Just make sure you give me the best bullets and the good ammunition to fight for you guys."

In the end, though, Ozzie knows it's always up to the player. The player is the one at the plate facing the hulking pitcher with the fastball that comes with its own vapor trail. The player is the one on the mound in the ninth inning with the winning run staring at him from third base. The manager? The manager hopes and prays.

The problems in Chicago seem far away and long ago as the spring-training games are set to begin. Oney Guillen, who had been a burr under the White Sox' saddle, is on the field in Jupiter, helping with the Marlins' workouts. So is his older brother, Ozzie Jr. The youngest brother, Ozney, is playing baseball for a community college in Miami. Their father looks younger and happier as he gets ready for another season. His wife, Ibis, already has told him he has his smile back.

The last few years in Chicago had been miserable. Now, White Sox general manager Kenny Williams is in Guillen's rearview mirror. Ozzie knows he's wanted in Miami. Being wanted is all he ever wanted.

There are lessons in the Guillen-Williams breakup for the Marlins.

"You have to be cognizant of everything in this business, whether you're bringing in a player that has a history like a Zambrano or something else is going on," Larry Beinfest says. "You need to at least do your homework. Knowing Ozzie and knowing the way he works and a little bit about his personality, I think you have a comfort level there. Whatever happened happened. That's between Ozzie and Kenny and the White Sox. We'll turn the page here in Miami."

It's time for a new chapter. Who knows, maybe Guillen will manage up a bit more this time around and find common ground with Beinfest. But the important thing is that, however he's managing—up, down, or sideways—he's now doing it with a smile on his face.

Lots of young players are in camp, and Guillen sees them as candidates to be molded in his image, the way Jon Garland and Aaron Rowand were in Chicago. *Play the game the right way.* It's what he learned years ago from Tom Seaver and Carlton Fisk and what he's passing on now with such gusto. Play the game right, or else—"or else" meaning he'll tell all to the media.

But throwing someone under the bus is the furthest thing from Ozzie's mind on Monday, March 5, 2012. The Marlins are taking on the St. Louis Cardinals in Guillen's first spring-training game as Miami's manager. Unwanted drama is nowhere in the vicinity. Life still looks shiny and new. Anything seems possible. The Marlins go on to win 4–3. Peace reigns. For the time being.

ACKNOWLEDGMENTS

In January 2011, I sent a book proposal to David Black, one of the big names among nonfiction literary agents. I had taken a swing at two novels with zero success, and so I did what agent after agent had suggested I do: I wrote about what I knew, which was sports.

My proposal centered on a famous former athlete. The details don't matter now. David's response does. After an e-mail exchange, we set up a time to talk by telephone. I called. His assistant transferred me. There was no preamble when David came on the line.

"Why would I want to read about [Famous Former Athlete]?" he said.

Well, I explained, Famous Former Athlete had lived an interesting life and had a compelling story full of ups and downs, intrigue, legal trouble, and so on.

"What about Ozzie Guillen?" David said.

What about Ozzie Guillen? We in Chicago knew him as a bigger-than-life character, but was that life big enough to interest a wide audience? David immediately saw all of Ozzie's different layers and knew that what stood out about the manager was that he didn't fit inside any neat package. He wasn't like any other leader, and David wondered if there might be a book in Guillen's unorthodox approach to baseball.

It took me a few days before I slapped my forehead and reached a conclusion. Of course Ozzie Guillen. What could I have been thinking? I knew him, I knew his work, and I knew that if anyone were looking for a book about a person who was full of life and opinions, Ozzie would be hard to beat. The fact that his first name—just *Ozzie*—suffices when talking about him anywhere convinced me there was an audience.

Thus *Ozzie's School of Management* was born, using a Ten Commandments format you might find in a business self-help book, only turned on its ear.

In the end, Famous Former Athlete had no chance.

Thank you, David. You have perfect aim.

I'm indebted to many people who supported me throughout the process of writing this book. Authors Ian O'Connor, Gene Wojciechowski, Michael Rosenberg, and Rick Telander (my column-writing compadre at the *Chicago Sun-Times*) were gracious enough to give their time and expertise to a book-writing rookie. I'd say I owe them, but I'd be afraid they'd take me up on it.

Another friend and colleague, Joe "Little C" Cowley, steered me down the right path with Ozzie on more than one occasion. The *Sun-Times*'s White Sox beat writer Daryl Van Schouwen was helpful and extremely patient with me.

Many players, executives, and other assorted baseball people were generous with their time, among them Manny Crespo, Jim Zerilla, Kenny Williams, Paul Konerko, A. J. Pierzynski,

Will Ohman, Omar Vizquel, Adam Dunn, Juan Pierre, Mark Buehrle, Gordon Beckham, Sergio Santos, Brent Lillibridge, Brent Morel, and Alex Rios. Many thanks to John Kruk, Jon Garland, John Danks, and any other Johns I'm forgetting. I'd also like to thank Ozzie Guillen Jr. for giving me insight into his father.

Chris De Luca, my sports editor at the *Sun-Times*, signed off on my writing this book and helped me along the way, and for that I'm very appreciative. I'm even more appreciative that I have him for a boss. I'm also grateful to John Barron, Don Hayner, and Andrew Herrmann for fostering an environment where good sports journalism matters.

Paul Golob, my editor at Times Books, added his wisdom to the process, without which this book would never have been written. He was a pro under a very tight deadline.

Eric White, Joe Goddard, Dan McGrath, Mike Downey, Allison Hemphill, and Emi Ikkanda are just some of the people who lent a hand along the way.

I couldn't have done this without my family. My wife, Anne, understood that, if I was going to write a book in addition to four columns a week for the *Sun-Times*, I was going to be locked in my office a lot. Now that I look back on it, she seemed to welcome this with an enthusiasm normally seen only in college cheerleaders. Okay, that's not true, but had she known how much I'd end up talking about the book's progress, she might have locked me in that office for good. I'm thankful for her love and belief. My children, Colleen, Eddie, and Charlie, have given me more than they could ever know, much of it in laughter.

I'd also like to thank my siblings for their support over the years, but two of them, Tom and Joanne, have been especially supportive of my attempts at book writing over the years. My late mother, Dorothy Morrissey, encouraged all seven of us to read, and we are better for it.

Most of all, I'd like to thank Ozzie Guillen. I asked a lot of questions and he answered every one of them. More than a few times, I told him to let me know if I was wearing him out, and I'd back off. Not necessary, he said; he'd tell me if I became a nuisance. He never did.

It took me about half the 2011 season to realize that, as much as I preferred one-on-one interviews with Guillen, his quotes were usually better when he was addressing a group of people. He loves a crowd. I got plenty of good material from him when we sat and talked alone, but he was much more alive when he was in front of people, plural.

I'm going to miss him, as are most of the writers in Chicago. But no matter how far away he is he'll be heard. Of this, I'm certain.

INDEX

ABOUT THE AUTHOR

RICK MORRISSEY is an award-winning sports columnist for the *Chicago Sun-Times*, and he has previously worked at the *Chicago Tribune*, the *Rocky Mountain News*, and the *Charlotte Observer.* He has covered most of the major events in sports, from the Super Bowl to the Olympics to the NBA Finals. He lives in the Chicago area.